Dedication

To my Minister, the Honorable Minister Louis Farrakhan. We love you and hope you will accept our work. Our souls delight in serving you! You have done your job so well and so exquisitely that we deserve the chastisement if we fall in this hour.

Preface

This is a book about Life Tips. Who wouldn't want to know Life Tips in an hour like this? There is so much more that all of us can do and should do to be more successful in this day and time. We wrote this book for you to reflect over and then get up and do. This is a very serious book that will inspire you to have the kind of life you want. We encourage you to read a tip or two a day and try them out and see how they work for you. We are very proud of you and we hope we can to you as a man and as a woman. God bless you!

- Brother Marcus and Sister Cecelia

Life Tips

Volume 1

LIFE IS ABOUT MOMENTS.

Create them.
Don't wait
for them.

Tip # 1

Prioritize tasks that move the needle

When it comes to getting things done, cross off tasks on your to do lists. Making a short list of maybe 3-5 tasks that if they were to get done, would really move the needle as far as getting you closer to your bigger picture goals. You can call this your "non-negotiables" list. Then make a list of 5-7 smaller tasks. Things that are not as significant or "needle moving," mostly just random chores and errands that you would still like to get done. Approach your non-negotiables as musts and put a little more pressure on yourself to get these things done. When it comes to the second list, you may not have a big of a sense of urgency.

If you get these extra things done – great! It's like a bonus and you should feel extra productive & accomplished. If you don't get them done, it's no big deal and you can simply migrate them over to the next day.

This sort of approach can make a big difference when it comes to the progress and growth you make towards your bigger goals.

Maybe you were making baby steps before but now you're making leaps and strides towards your dream life.

If you're busy all the time and have trouble getting everything you want done, try focusing on the tasks that move your needle instead of keeping yourself preoccupied with busy work.

Tip # 2

Cut out Excessive Leisure

Download an app on your phone that tracks how much you use your phone – how many times you unlock it and how many hours a day you spend on it.

When you remembered to check it, you will be shocked! You might think that on average you would log between 2-3 hours a day, but you might find that you clock upwards of 3-5 hours a day, and some days will be as high as 8 hours. Yes 8 whole hours on your phone, in one day.

Honestly, that's ridiculous.

And might we add that this doesn't even include the amount of time you spend on your laptop and I pad everyday – searching the internet, online shopping, or watching YouTube and Netflix.

I hate to ever be too hard on myself. But I have so many goals that Sometimes we've been at this thing for so long that when we see that we're spending so many hours in a day on our phone, we can't help but feel a tiny bit disappointed in ourselves.

We're heavy advocates for rest and relaxation. We hate the stigma around goal chasing that and being #teamnosleep and grinding it out 24/7 is somehow an indication that you're serious about your dreams.

But we also know that lack of time is a major excuse a lot of people use for not going after the kind of life they want. We're learning more and more that we always have time. Contrary to popular belief, there are enough hours in the day. It's just about how we use those hours.

How many times have we been running late for work, but still managed to make time to stop and get our morning coffee?

We make time for the things we want to make time for.

If something truly matters and is a priority for us – we WILL find a way to make it happen.

Look at your day to day activities and see if you're wasting precious time anywhere.

The point is to cut back, not cut out.

So, maybe just watch 2 episodes of the new season of Breaking Bad instead of binging the whole thing in one sitting. Or catch up on just one vlog from your favorite youtuber, instead of watching 25 apartment tours.

Instead of accepting a reality where it seems like you just can't get anything done – make your goals a daily priority. Replace some of the excessive leisure with productive work that gets you closer to the kind of life you want to live.

Tip # 3

Wake up Earlier

We know that some of you may already be early birds, but there are others who'll skip over this section and think that waking up earlier isn't going to make that big of a difference.

Waking up earlier may seem like super common sense to some, but maybe you feel that your a night owl.

Maybe you stay up anywhere from 2 - 4 o' clock in the morning, get up at 12 o'clock and leave me just enough time to do the necessities (shower, eat, etc.) before having to leave for work.

Maybe your telling myself that it was fine because you were "more productive" at night anyway – and you kind of were, to some extent. The reality, however, was that you felt like you never were getting as much done, as you wanted to.

After working a full shift and long commute, it was tough to try and sit at your desk and get focused enough to work on your own projects. You would always be so exhausted from work & lacking motivation at the end of the day that you were only ever able to get done the bare minimum. This, in turn, meant that you were never making the kind of progress you wanted to on your bigger goals.

Maybe this time you'll heed some good advice. Wake up earlier and go to bed at a sensible hour.

You will be able to tell the difference in the way you feel and how much you will be able to get things done and how many of your goals you hit!

If you're having trouble hitting your goals or feel you just never have enough time to get things done – try waking up earlier.

You'll see a major difference in your productivity and ability to get things done when you give yourself some extra time in the mornings dedicated specifically to creating your dream life.

One of the key habits of successful people is having an effective morning routine. Successful people plan everything including their mornings the night before.

They wake up with determination, ready to start another great day that will get them one step closer on the path to their goals.

There are many advantages to being an early riser. Early risers have been shown to be more successful and often in better shape which will lead to increased productivity.

Tip # 4

Be awake

Once you get used to being productive you will value sleep more. When you are awake, be awake 2.0. That means you treat your waking hours like you are making up for the time you've spent asleep. You want to do so much in your day that when your head hits your pillow at night, your exhausted and feel you've earned the right to catch some z's.

Be awake 2.0.

Earning your sleep at the end of the day, makes so much more sense than only allowing yourself 3-5 hours of rest a night – because that's somehow a badge of honor that you're "grinding."

So, yes, wake up earlier. But spend the hours you are awake wisely and productively & earn your sleep at the end of the day, so you can continue to kick behind the next.

THINGS TO DO WHEN YOU
HAVE A HEADACHE

DRINK WATER

EAT WATERMELON

APPLY ICE TO
YOUR TEMPLES

DRINK A CUP
OF COFFEE

MASSAGE PEPPERMINT OIL
ONTO YOUR TEMPLES

EAT SOMETHING SPICY

DRINK
GINGER TEA

CLICK TO GET MORE TIPS

PureWow.

Tip # 5

Invest in online courses

It's basically like taking on another full-time job when you decide to take the pursuit of your dreams seriously.

To have life coming at you on the day to day + whatever newfound responsibilities you get from your side projects – the overwhelm and anxiety can start to kick in fast.

You'll save yourself a ton of time and stress if you invest in things like online courses to acquire the skills you need as opposed to spending months or even years going through the trial and error phases.

Someone has been right where you are and is willing to give you all their secrets in exchange for payment – saving you tons of frustration, stress, and most importantly time.

It will be hard to stop taking them once you get used to the convenience of being able to learn anything you want from the comfort of your home.

Some people buy a bunch of individual online courses in the past – sometimes spending more than a thousand dollars for one course. There are many platforms out there like Skillshare. What people like about Skillshare is that it makes pursuing any curiosities or interests you have possible. And you don't have to deal with the inconvenience of leaving your home to go to a classroom or worry about paying ungodly amounts of tuition.

You get access to a variety of courses on (almost) any subject you can think of at an affordable monthly price ($15/m).

Think of that. You can learn another language for that amount. Almost anything you want to learn is available for you in the form of comprehensive courses and guides. You don't have much to lose & you can cancel it at any time.

Tip # 6

Discipline and consistency are the keys to (Literally everything)

Without commitment you'll never start. But more importantly, without consistency, you'll never finish. Everything you want is on the other side of how disciplined you choose to be. Everything.

Whenever you've researched any sort of tips on goal setting, consistency is always top of the list. And for good reason.

We want to encourage you to not just dabble in the things that interest you. Dabbling here and there doesn't get us anywhere. Committing to mastery is where real progress is made.

If you take nothing else from this book, please understand that developing self-discipline and staying consistent are the most important things in life.

Progress may sometimes feel slow when you're in the thick of it. But forming the habit of acting is what matters.

When you show up for your life, even when you lack the motivation to do so, you develop this unwavering grit. The kind of grit where you know that even if everything messes up, you can always start anew.

You, and you alone, are responsible for your life. The sooner we accept that fact, the sooner we can go about the business of transforming our lives.

Tip # 7

Work on Financial Literacy

Money is one of those super taboo topics. Everyone (usually) wants more of it but at the same time is super secretive and private about it. From our experience, people seem to get weird and uncomfortable when the topic of money & finances comes up.

We can say from experience that a lot of problems we've faced in the past wouldn't have been problems if we would have had better managed our money.

Financial freedom brings peace of mind. Anything that brings peace of mind is the ultimate form of self-care. Not everyone wants to be a billionaire, but it's also no fun living paycheck to paycheck indefinitely.

When we say financial literacy, we mean managing your money in a way that allows you to live your life fully without worrying about money or bills.

That looks different for everyone but getting out of debt, living below your means, and saving money are standard practices that can benefit anyone no matter what their current financial situation looks like.

If money has been a point of stress for you, try living minimally, budgeting, and upping your savings as a form of self-care that builds the foundation for the kind of life you want to have.

Tip # 8

Take up Journaling

Keeping a journal is one of the best moves you can make it your life. It helps you to keep track of how you are doing now. It is a good reminder to take the process one day at a time.

Journaling is probably the most impactful thing you ever could incorporate into your life.

There's something about being able to put your unfiltered thoughts and feelings down on paper that is so clarifying and therapeutic. Maybe you've never kept a journal before. We recommend trying it out at least once. There are so many different types of journals you can try out to see which method works best for you.

There's the ever-popular bullet journaling, there's gratitude journaling, there's journaling for wealth and abundance, and so many more. But if you open your notebook and never know what to say, using prompts is a great place to start.

Some people use a method called a stream of consciousness journaling (aka just writing down everything that comes to mind as it comes). It brings a lot of clarity because you're essentially dumping everything that's on your mind onto paper.

It gives you room to think clearly and critically about your life & allows space for your creativity to flow.

Tip # 9

Pursue Passion Projects and Chase your curiosity
You must go after the things that make you come alive.
Every day you must find things that bring meaning to your life.
We've spent most of our adult lives working at jobs we've hated and couldn't wait to quit. There are some jobs we hate more than other jobs. More than anything though, was that we don't have anything else going for ourselves apart from work. We may be studying for something and it's so boring it leaves you feeling even more unfulfilled and miserable. Maybe you unable to quit your current job.
The difference is always that your life outside of work can be much more fulfilling with your hobbies and things that you really look forward to.
What us your main creative hobby? What do you love doing?
If you're not sure about hobbies or passions you want to pursue, we recommend following your curiosity.
Not everyone knows what they're passionate about, but everyone is curious about something and if you're not then you've got some reevaluating to do.
Most of the things that you might be good at won't be realized because they're too boring and they are not sexy enough for you.
Some of the problem is we are so boring and don't want to do anything. You must investigate things for yourself and then make a good decision. When was the last time you let your curiosity take over? When was the last time you didn't have anything to lose when it came to learning something about something? It's not like we have much else going on? You want to be interested in other people and what they do instead of trying to be interesting.
If you're having a hard time finding a creative niche or genre that you like, we recommend moving in the direction of your curiosity until you find the thing that sticks.

Tip # 10

Budget

Budgets can help you improve your finances almost immediately. With a budget, you track your money coming in (your income) against your money going out (your expenses). If you want to do this and implement a budget, you can feel less money stress every month and start having money for things you want to do in life.

Once you create your first budget, begin to use it and get a good feel for how it can keep your finances on track, you may want to map out your spending plan or budget for 6 months to a year down the road. By doing this you can easily forecast which months your finances may be tight and which ones you'll have extra money. You can then look for ways to even out the highs and lows in your finances so that things can be more manageable and pleasant.

Extending your budget out into the future also allows you to forecast how much money you will be able to save for important things like your vacation, a new vehicle, your first home or home renovations, an emergency savings account or your retirement. Using a realistic budget to forecast your spending for the year can really help you with your long-term financial planning. You can then make realistic assumptions about your annual income and expense and plan for long term financial goals like starting your own business, buying an investment or recreation property or retiring.

Financial freedom starts with your budget! It's that important.

Tip # 11

Don't buy lotto tickets

Lotto tickets are not a good investment. You're more likely to be struck by lightning than to win the lotto, yet many people continue to spend money buying weekly lotto tickets. Have you ever been stuck in a long line at the gas station and you were there to purchase gas and everyone there was there for the lottery?

Also, if you do manage to beat the odds, studies show that your happiness only spikes briefly after winning the lotto but returns to pre-winning levels within just a few months. Happiness levels of lotto winners are not significantly higher than non-winners. Instead of thinking that the only way to become rich is to win the lotto — become a person of action, take the appropriate risks and plan your financial future.

Tip # 12

life hacks   #2525

How long should you nap for?

10-20 minutes - To boost alertness, energy, and a good way to refresh and get back to work.

30 minutes - Never! Studies show these leave you feeling extrememly groggy.

60 minutes - To improve your fact, face, and name recognition.

90 minutes - To improve emotional, procedural memory and creativity. Also the easiest to wake up from.

@1000LifeHacks
1000LifeHacks.com

Tip # 13

Drive a safe and reliable car

A luxury car might sound nice and even if you could afford it, it's not a very practical or budget-savvy choice. A luxury car usually comes with paying extra for premium gas and luxury-priced repairs.

This isn't necessarily a bad thing, but it could eat up a large portion of your budget. Frugal people tend to drive safe and reliable cars, not only because they are more affordable up front, but they cost less money in the long run.

Tip # 14

Carry just enough cash with you

If carrying a credit card is too tempting for you, or you have trouble paying your bill each month – switch to a cash budget instead. When visiting the grocery store, make a detailed list and carry only enough cash to cover what you need to buy. This forces you to plan your purchases in advance and avoid unnecessary spending.

Tip # 15

Use a credit card with good rewards

If you are good at paying off your total credit card bill each month, then we highly recommend getting one that offers rewards. There are many different ones available today with no annual fee that offer great rewards.

Whether it's cash-back, movie points, restaurants points or travel points, there is sure to be one available that suits your interests. Some people feel that they are likely to spend more money when using plastic, but maybe you'll tend to spend less this way and avoid high interest fees because you will always pay off your bill in full each month.

Tip # 16

Don't shop as a form of entertainment

Remember when you used to hang out with your friends at the mall. It was something to do, especially during the winter when it was too cold to go outside.

But hanging out at the mall usually leads to unnecessary spending – whether you buy clothes, shoes, makeup or a snack at the food court – this impulsive spending can hurt your budget.

Instead of viewing shopping as a form of entertainment, only shop when you need something. It's OK to browse the stores occasionally but avoid this if you have trouble with impulse spending.

Tip # 17

Repair and reuse what you can

We live in a society where we are made to feel the need to have the latest phone, the latest fashion, or the latest car even though last year's model is still in working condition. Frugal people don't fall for these marketing tactics. Instead they make the most of what they already have. They mend their clothes, fix their appliances and maintain their car instead of jumping to get a replacement. Frugal people don't compare themselves to the Joneses – they don't even think about them. If you don't know how to do something, learn it. You google everything else. Who wants to be ignorant?

Tip # 18

Live in a modest home

Just because the bank says you can afford a given mortgage doesn't mean you should listen to their advice. Opt for a house that fits your needs and comfort level instead of buying a bigger and nicer one than you need.
Since housing costs are usually a huge percentage of one's household budget, be realistic when choosing where to live.
Maybe renting is a better option than buying, that's why it's important to factor in all the costs and weigh the pros and cons to decide which choice is right for your budget.

Tip # 19

Cook food at home

You should never have a favorite restaurant. Not when you can cook. If you don't know how to cook go to www.nfastudios.com and learn how to. The best advice we can give anyone is to learn how to make at least three delicious meals at home. That way you'll be able to whip up something nice if you have friends coming over, or you want to have a relaxing evening at home.
This is much more affordable than getting take out or eating in a restaurant where you must leave a tip.

If possible, try to make food from scratch, it's almost always cheaper and healthier than processed or pre-packaged food. I know that many of us are short on time, which is why we recommend spending an afternoon or morning on the weekend preparing meals for the following week.

Tip # 20

Make more money

You need to make enough money meet your financial goals. If you're not doing this from your day job, then figure out how to make extra money on the side. Say yes to more hours at work; work toward a bonus; pick up a side job; start an online business. Whatever you do, do something! Whatever you do, find ways to make more money every month so you can reach your financial goals. Don't let your lack of income be the excuse you use to stay broke. You must have money if you want to get married. You must have money if you want to stay married.

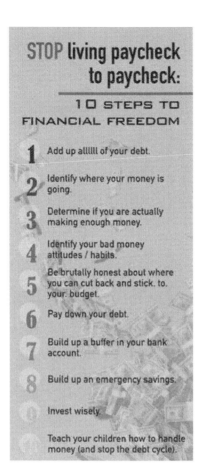

STOP living paycheck to paycheck:

10 STEPS TO FINANCIAL FREEDOM

1 Add up alllll of your debt.

2 Identify where your money is going.

3 Determine if you are actually making enough money.

4 Identify your bad money attitudes / habits.

5 Be brutally honest about where you can cut back and stick. to. your. budget.

6 Pay down your debt.

7 Build up a buffer in your bank account.

8 Build up an emergency savings.

9 Invest wisely.

10 Teach your children how to handle money (and stop the debt cycle).

Tip # 21

Enjoy Staying at home

Going out usually costs money. We're not suggesting that you spend your evenings and weekends like a hermit where you never go outside, but a better suggestion is to plan if you do decide to go out. Have dinner before meeting friends or invite them over for drinks and light snacks instead of spending money at a bar. If you do go out, check to see if any dinner deals or coupons are available. If you have a day off though, why not spend the day at home relaxing with your family, friend or spouse instead of paying a fortune for admission and popcorn at the theatres.

Think long-term when making decisions

One of the main differences between people who are frugal and people who are "cheap", is that cheap people think short term, while frugal people think long term.

Before spending money on anything non-essential, it's important to access the short-term vs. long-term benefits of your potential purchase. After the short-term benefits fade, that money spent is gone.

However, if you are willing to sacrifice some of those short-term benefits for long-term gains, the reward will almost always be bigger and better.

Tip # 22

Buy quality instead of quantity

Instead of buying cheap fashion that is often trendy and likely to fall apart after one season, invest in well-made pieces that are timeless and will last for years to come.

We have found this tip important, especially for shoes. We bought a pair of sandals at K & G and the strap broke the first time Marcus wore them.

That was the last time Marcus bought shoes from K & G and now prefer to invest in quality shoes that are comfortable and built to last.

Instead of having a closet full of cheaper shoes, we would rather own less shoes but make sure they are quality pairs.

Apply the same rule when making any big purchase. Don't necessarily gravitate towards the cheapest item on the shelf.

Sometimes for food products or toiletries we opt for the store brands, but when it comes to technology or appliances, it's important to do your research first and go with the brand that is well-made and reliable.

Look for Deals and clip coupons

Whenever possible, avoid paying full price for anything. Instead make a little effort to find deals, clip coupons and get the best value for your money.

Many celebrities have been reported to clip coupons as part of their routine. Despite your income level, looking for deals just makes sense.

Tip # 24

Use everything up to the last drop

Were not ashamed to admit that we are those people that cut open our bottle of body lotion in order to scoop out the last bit of moisturizer.

It's not that we are cheap, we just don't like to see anything go to waste. Also, you'd be surprised at how much product is left in the bottle when most people think it's done.

Using up everything to the last drop prevents unnecessary waste and saves you money as it all adds up in the long run.

Tip # 25

Have an emergency Fund

Unfortunately, today, there really is no job security. We hear about it in the news that companies are trimming down their employees or restructuring which could mean layoffs or pay cuts.

No matter what your income level is, it's essential to put aside an emergency fund. This means living below your means, saving money and making smart investments.

Here are a few ideas to help you save and make money:

Start a blog

Blogging is a wonderful hustle because the start-up costs are low, and it can be a great way to make extra money in your spare time. Blogging even has the potential to turn into a full-time job.

Freelance writing

This is a popular way to make money online and it's great if you enjoy writing.

Earn Cashback

Maybe you like shopping on **Ebates** so you can cashback on all your purchases. You can also use **Checkout 51** to earn cashback when grocery shopping. Both Ebates and Checkout 51 are free to join.

Online surveys

There are many online survey websites that will pay you to complete surveys, play games, do online searches and more. They are free to sign up for and free to use. Survey websites we recommend include **Swagbucks, American Consumer Opinion, Panel Place** and **QuickRewards**.

Become an Airbnb host

If you have a cabin, cottage or extra room in your home, consider becoming an Airbnb host to make extra money. Don't have any extra space? You can choose to become a host for your neighborhood or make money by hosting a unique experience (hiking, cooking classes, and more).

Tip # 26

HOW TO REMOVE PERMANENT MARKER FROM EVERYTHING

CLOTHES – USE HAND SANITIZER

WALLS – USE TOOTHPASTE OR HAIRSPRAY

WOOD – USE RUBBING ALCOHOL

CARPET – USE WHITE VINEGAR

FURNITURE – USE MILK

WHITE BOARD – USE DRY ERASE MARKER OR PENCIL RUBBER ERASER

CERAMIC OR GLASS – USE 1 PART TOOTHPASTE WITH 1 PART BAKING SODA

Tip # 27

We all know how terrible anxiety can feel. From the nauseous feeling before you give a presentation, to the panicky sensation when you must try something new, to the overwhelming anxiety that incapacitates you.

Grounding is a simple but effective therapeutic technique that can help you when strong anxiety hits. You can use grounding when you feel like the anxiety is taking over, when you feel numb, like you are in a dream, lost in past events, or having an out-of-body or out-of-reality experience.

Grounding helps to bring a person back to the here and now, to realize that they are safe and in control of their reality and emotions. It helps a person to refocus and find calmness and strength in the present moment when they are highly anxious and emotional. There are many different grounding techniques for anxiety and the following 5 ways are some of our favorites:

Grounding techniques for anxiety
The 54321 technique.
Name 5 things you can see in the room with you (e.g. chair, painting)
Name 4 things you can feel (e.g. my feet on the floor, cool air on my skin)
Name 3 things you can hear right now (e.g. people talking outside)
Name 2 things you can smell right now (e.g. toast, perfume)
Name 1 good thing about yourself (e.g. I am strong)

Tip # 28

Touch and describe an object
Find an object around you e.g. cushion, handbag, water bottle. Try to describe it as if you are explaining it to someone who has never seen it before. e.g.
"This is a cushion, it is a square shape with a red and purple pattern of stripes…it feels soft with some hard ridges around the corners"
Repeat until you feel calm.

Tip # 29

Memory game
When you are feeling anxious, you need to try to reorient yourself to the present moment and using declarative memory can help with this. e.g.
Name as many types of dog breeds you can.
How many cities have you visited around the world?
Repeat the alphabet backwards.

TRUE ASSERTIVENESS
How to influence people

Your body language is a powerful ally when you need to be assertive. Use it effectively and your dynamism becomes contagious. You will find that people start to single you out so they can listen to what you have to say.

RULE #1
Eyes

Your eyes are the most expressive part of your face. You should use them as much as possible. They have the ability to convey emotions such as interest, concern, warmth and credibility. Imagine talking to someone wearing sunglasses. It's much harder to read their feelings when you can't see their eyes.

RULE #2
Hands

Let your hands do what comes naturally. The trick is to try to relax. The natural action is for your hands to move as you talk. This is why really confident and assertive people often look relaxed – their hands move naturally and in a coordinated way with their voice.

RULE #3
Smile

By smiling you also exude warmth and positivity. Be conscious of this when you meet people for the first time. It's worth making an effort to smile. You'll find that people will 'warm' to you more quickly. They're more likely to want to talk to you and listen to what you have to say.

RULE #4
Expression

Using your face to its maximum advantage is an essential part of being assertive. It helps to make you look and feel more confident. Use your face to give non-verbal cues. Using your facial expressions effectively also helps you to clarify your message and communicate your emotion.

RULE #5
Voice

Try to make a conscious effort to modulate your tone. Varying your tone keeps your voice engaging. It should help you to sound more enthusiastic too. Enthusiasm is contagious. If you sound enthusiastic, there's much more chance other people will listen. They will feel enthusiastic about you.

RULE #6
Silence

It sounds odd to say but using silences in your speech can actually help you to come across more assertively; if people are expecting you to say something and yet they see that you seem comfortable with the silence, you'll look more confident and in control.

AND FINALLY...

Being assertive means practising whenever you get the chance. Don't just wait for opportunities to come along. Actively seek out chances to try out the assertiveness skills I've introduced you to. You can't become more assertive by sitting back and hoping for the best.

Tip # 30

Say your mantra

When you are not in an anxious state, it can be helpful to develop a list of personal mantras or affirmations that help you when you become panicked or disoriented. Write them down somewhere and keep them in your handbag. e.g.

I am safe, I am here in the present moment

This feeling will pass, nothing bad is happening right now

I can handle these emotions, I am strong

Tip # 31

Square Breathing

Getting your breathing under control can be hugely effective in reducing anxiety, but most people either breathe too fast or hold their breath when they are trying to calm down. Square breathing is a simple way to refocus your attention to your breath and the present moment.

With your index finger, slowly trace the shape of a square in front of you, keeping your eyes on that finger.

With one side, breathe in for 3 seconds...

With the next side, hold your breath for 1 second...

With the third side, breathe out for 3 seconds...

With the final side, hold for 1 second...

Tip # 32

Set Financial Goals

You need to set financial goals if you want to change your finances. Examples of goals can be to get out of debt, pay off your student loans, or save for a new car.

Whatever your financial goals are, make sure you write them down and use the SMART method of goal setting to learn exactly how to set goals.

In the meantime, just know that goals should be:

Specific
Measurable
Actionable
Realistic
Timely

Your financial goals will move you from where you are now to where you want to go. Without them, it can feel impossible to make progress financially.

Tip # 33

Realize that happiness doesn't mean having everything you want and being problem-free all the time.
We cannot control everything that happens to us in life, but we can choose how we respond. When we respond with an attitude of 'Why is this happening to me?' and adopt a victim mentality, we suffer. When we choose to respond with an attitude of 'Why is this happening for me and what can I learn?' then we feel a lot more empowered, which impacts our mental state positively.
The biggest misconception about happiness is that we can outsource it — that something external is going to make us happy. Happiness is NOT a constant state. As humans we experience and grow through a variety of emotions. The expectation that we should be happy all the time will leave anyone with an expectation hangover. What we can be is grateful.

Tip # 34

Cut **"should"** from your vocabulary, because it basically guarantees whatever you think "should" happen, won't.
When we use the word 'should,' it's like this big, judgmental finger wagging at yourself. 'I should work out more, I should be happier, I should be more grateful.' It causes us to feel guilt and shame. It depletes our happiness. It causes us to engage in behaviors that are completely against what we want.
Instead, replace 'should' with 'I would like.' For example, 'I'd like to lose weight, because I want to have more energy and be a role model.' That is more motivational, it's more based on passion rather than the fear and judgment of ourselves that prevents us from being the people that we want to be.

Tip # 35

Remember that your negative thoughts are not true. They're just thoughts.

Sadly, many people make the mistake of believing the negative things that their 'inner voice' tells them, often without even being aware of their right to question whether these things are accurate! When it comes to mental health care, many people still think you will need to spend years exploring your childhood or past in order to get better. That's simply not the case nowadays. Catch, challenge, and change negative thoughts. Get audited and come up the bridge quickly!

Tip # 36

Start your day by reminding yourself one positive thing about your life. This can be a small observation like enjoying beautiful weather or something more profound like recognizing you have achieved one step towards a life goal (working in the industry you always dreamt of, have a best friend who you are grateful for, etc.). We tend to hold onto negatives a lot stronger than the positives, so this can be a small way to give yourself a moment to check in with the 'happier' thoughts and realities.

Tip # 37

Anyone can benefit from therapy, so consider making an appointment for a checkup. There is a stereotype that many people have about the unique person who chooses to see a therapist. 'They must be an emotional wreck,' or 'they can't take care of their own problems,' or 'they must be crazy.' That last one is probably the most popular and worst misconception of them all!

It takes a lot of insight and emotional awareness to realize that you want to enlist the services of a trained mental health therapist to get the right help you need. Yes, there are some clients who seek therapy when they are at the absolute lowest emotional point in their lives, but there are also just as many who simply want to become emotionally healthier people to enhance their work and intimate relationships. No problem is too small or large when you come to see one of us. It's all welcomed because our job is to meet you where you are at in life, not where we or anyone else thinks you should be.

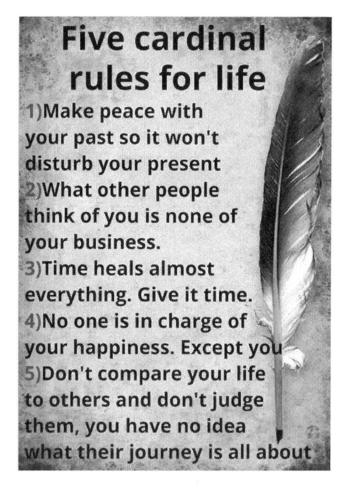

Five cardinal rules for life

1) Make peace with your past so it won't disturb your present
2) What other people think of you is none of your business.
3) Time heals almost everything. Give it time.
4) No one is in charge of your happiness. Except you
5) Don't compare your life to others and don't judge them, you have no idea what their journey is all about

Tip # 38

Don't think about your work responsibilities at home, and vice versa

Be present when present, which requires dropping the guilt. Guilt has no benefits for anyone. When you are at work, stay focused, when you are home, give [it] your undivided attention. Doing your best in each place will keep you sane and feeling good about your output.

Tip # 39

Stop checking your smartphone randomly. Instead, give yourself specific times to catch up on social media and email.

Most people would be happier (and less stressed) if they checked their phone less. A study of college students at Kent State University found that people who check their phones frequently tend to experience higher levels of distress during their leisure time when they intend to relax!

Instead of willing ourselves to just check less often, we can configure our devices and work time so that we are tempted less often. The goal is to check email, social media, and messages on your phone just a few times a day — intentionally, not impulsively.

Our devices are thus returned to their status as tools we use strategically — not slot machines that randomly demand our energy and attention.

Tip # 40

Make keeping up with your friendships a priority

People think that when work or school or family responsibilities get busy, then hanging out with your friends becomes a luxury that must be cut. It's often the first thing to go, even if people are still going to the gym or binge-watching whatever's new on Netflix. Making sure to spend time with your friends has enormous mental health benefits and keeps your stress level in check. It's a great coping mechanism and a necessity for your health that should not be cut when things get tough — on the contrary, you need it more than ever.

Tip # 41

Take the time to plan short-term pleasure AND long-term goals — aka actively make your life what you want it to be.
A lot of people rush around without devoting a few minutes each week to reflecting and strategizing. We may all recognize we've periodically contemplated signing up to volunteer at Big Brother Big Sister, then totally forget. Or we mean to switch jobs and then procrastinate, then we're facing our second year in a position we planned to quickly exit.
When we don't purposefully and deliberately choose where to focus our energies and times, other people — our bosses, our colleagues, our clients, and even our families — will choose for us, and before long we'll have lost sight of everything that is meaningful and important.
Spend time each week planning — plan activities you may enjoy in the moment and think bigger, considering what you want long term.

Tip # 42

Treat yourself with compassion and lots of love.
People believe that self-care is selfish, so they avoid doing things that are necessities. Self-love, self-care, and self-fulfillment. It's a lot of self, because happiness starts from within. Self-love includes eliminating negative self-talk and accepting yourself, flaws and all. Self-care means setting boundaries and taking time to refill your energy. Self-fulfillment is all about living your values and having authentic relationships.

Tip # 43

Don't forget that your physical health has an impact on your mental health, too.
Some physical things you can do to create a habit of happiness: Honor your circadian rhythm by waking shortly after sunrise and going to sleep a few hours after sunset. Not only do we need seven to nine hours of sleep in order to be happy, but our brain functions better by sharing the rhythm of the sun.

Incorporate play into your life: Some easy ways to this are when you exercise, do something that makes you laugh, like a dance class, jumping on a trampoline, or playing a group sport.

Meditate. This can be as simple as an app [like] **Headspace**.

Tip # 44

Several times throughout your day, take a deep breath and tell yourself that everything is OK. Eventually, your brain will get the memo. The bills may be piling up with you having no idea of how they are going to get paid. Your mother may have Alzheimer's and dealing with that is wearing you out. You may be starting to wonder if there really is someone out there for you. BUT in this moment, your heart is beating, you're breathing, and you have food in your tummy and a roof over your head. Underneath all the circumstances, desires, and wants, you're OK. While fixing dinner, walking through the grocery store, driving to work, or reading emails, come into the present moment and remind your brain,

'I'm all right, right now.'

Over time with repetition, learning to come into the present and calming your brain and body will change the neural pathways in your brain — a scientific truth called neuroplasticity — so that this becomes the norm for you.

Tip # 45

Make a conscious effort to take care of your mental health the same way you would your physical health.

Too many people neglect to make their mental health a priority! And so, it gets forgotten about and put in the 'too-hard' or 'too-busy.' But just like physical health, mental health really should be considered non-negotiable because without it, we have nothing else.

If I had to limit the key ingredients to happiness and good mental health to just a few I'd say good quality relationships and connectedness, good physical health and well-being, living a life with meaning and purpose, loving oneself and others, and having a sense of hope and optimism for the future.

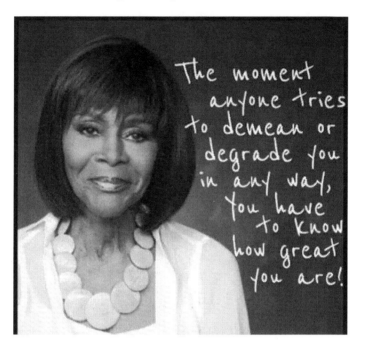

Tip # 46

Track your net worth

Start tracking your net worth to see where you are financially. Tracking your net worth is how you measure your overall financial health at a given time. It's a good indicator of where you stand financially today.

To track your net worth, use a net worth spreadsheet. This will get you in the habit of calculating your own net worth, instead of just using an online aggregator.

To track your net worth, subtract your liabilities from your assets (net worth = assets – liabilities).

Every month or quarter (whichever you want), update your net worth. This will show you how much your net worth is increasing (or decreasing!) over time.

If you want to have financial success, measuring your net worth is a must.

Tip # 47

Many people are not sure about what personal development means for them. Others understand the concept but don't know how to go about it. Both problems are easily addressed by gathering information about the subject. This book is full of great tips about personal development for all types of people.

Setting personal development goals means making yourself better, not perfect. Remember that the occasional mistake is inevitable. Treat mistakes as learning opportunities and do not be too afraid of them. Concentrate on how your next action will be improved by the knowledge gained from a mistake instead of worrying about repeating it.

Always try to improve yourself and your work. If you feel that you can be a better person or that something you do or work on could be better, then strive to apply that to the next tasks. By constantly trying to do better, you are trying to become a better person and a harder worker.

Personal development can be stressful, since it presents many challenges as you're looking to change old habits. Try to minimize stress in your life during this period. Minimizing stress can prevent overreacting to stressors. This will make every obstacle more likely to be an eventual success, since overreacting makes us more susceptible to missteps.

To increase your chances of success, learn from others' mistakes. There are many blogs, books and free seminars that you can attend that will help you set your own goals and guidelines. This helpful advice can give you direction and help you avoid mistakes; however, when you do make a mistake, and you will, learn from it and move on.

Come up with a little pep talk for yourself. Write down all your positive traits on a postcard. Carry this list with you always and take it out when you need to pick yourself up. Take it a step further and record yourself reading your list. Are you wondering why you should do this?

During difficult times – times when you are battling some personal weakness or failing – it is always best to stay busy. An occupied mind does not wander. If you let yourself sit quietly and just dwell and think about how bad the situation is, you will just feel worse. If you cannot do anything to improve the situation, it is better to spend time with friends, go out and get some exercise, and so on.

Make a detailed, thorough list of all your past and present accomplishments as they relate to home, school, work, and your health. Do not miss an opportunity to make additions to your list. Visit it every day to remind yourself of the importance of who you are and what you do, and how you can continue to add to the list.

Replace negative thoughts with ones that are more positive or balanced. Keep a journal of negative thoughts and what triggers them. When you are in a better mood, go over your journal and see if the negative thoughts you had were necessary and how you can change the way you viewed them at the time.

A self-help strategy for overcoming anxiety is to stop thinking in absolutes, using words like **"never," "always," "must,"** and so on. This type of distorted thinking results in unrealistic expectations, which cause you to put additional, excessive pressure on yourself. By defeating these cognitive distortions and putting thoughts into more realistic terms, you are less likely to overwhelm yourself with stress.

You should feel much more prepared for increasing your personal worth through development. Use this advice in your day to day life and you will quickly see your efficiency increasing. This can be applied as much to your personal life as it can to your professional life.

Tip # 48

Daily Alignment – It is so important to align yourself first thing in the morning so that your whole day flows smoother and in doing so you set yourself up for amazing things to come into your experience. Have a morning self-care routine that you do every day and it truly does make such a difference.

Tip # 49

Do everything from a place of love – especially if you are a parent. In some scenarios you will have a sink full of dishes and dinner needing to be made, etc. Do everything from a place of love. When you do it from love, it gives it more purpose and it puts you more in alignment with that which you want to receive.

the
10 COMMANDMENTS
of a
TIDY HOME

1) Let go of things (not just material things!)

2) Visualize a life free of clutter.

3) Keep only the things that spark joy.

4) Get rid of the things you'll use "someday."

5) Respect your home goods for the use they provide you.

6) Don't hold onto things for fear of the future.

7) Don't hold onto things to preserve the past.

8) Make an epic clean sweep.

9) Don't store items according to the season.

10) Don't let your possessions control you.

Tip # 50

Build your emergency Fund to last you for at least 6 months to a year

Financial experts recommend saving an emergency fund of six months to a year of discretionary expenses, or even more depending on your sources of income (if you have one source versus three sources every month). The one thing that we know for sure is that having an emergency fund takes away the fear around emergencies with respect to how you'll pay for them. The emergency still may stink, but you won't stress and worry about how you'll pay for it if you have money saved. And emergencies will happen. They happen to everyone.

Tip # 51

We are here to create – you have something to offer.

We were born to create. In other words, the world needs smart people to build things. We need employees who invent things, entrepreneurs who create things, and freelancers who design things. We need secretaries who make jewelry as a side project and stay-at-home dads who write amazing novels. We need more leaders, not more followers. We need more creators, not more consumers. And perhaps the most important thing to realize is that we not only need to create for each other, but for ourselves as well. Creating something is the perfect way to avoid wasting the precious moments that we have been given. To contribute, to create, to chip in to the world around you and to add your line to the world's story — that is a life well lived.

What will you create today?

Tip # 52

You dream the ideas that are meant to come through you; start before you're ready – oh my gosh I loved this one, it touched me so much. I don't know about you, but a lot of times I feel like a fraud, or like I'm not actually knowledgeable enough to write about anything I want to because who am I to write on a certain topic? Especially when I'm no expert. But, if a dream or an idea comes to you, it's because you are meant to bring it forward. You don't have to have a Ph.D. or 20 years' experience in something to begin sharing what you know. That's how you become an expert.

Tip # 53

Keep your new ideas to yourself. When you have a new idea, the energy around it is sacred to you. And when we share that energy before it's ready, we risk losing it. They related it like the steam coming out of a kettle; we need to hold our ideas in until they're ready, because we need the steam! Have you ever gotten an amazing idea, one that would be a big undertaking, and you shared it with someone and then felt a little bit of the steam lost? That's because when we talk about it, we create the energy that it's already happened, and it can make you lose momentum.

Tip # 54

You must act – don't wait until you think you're ready…if you have the vision, just start. Start the book, start the business, start whatever it is you've been dreaming about.

Acting is one of the most necessary steps in effectuating life changes. However, as most of us know, sometimes it is very difficult to take that first step and commit to a desired achievement.

So, what do you need to do in order to act? Motivation, you might say.

But, not so fast! There is a misconception that motivation is the reason for acting. The truth of the matter is that motivation is the result of action, not its cause. Thus, you don't need to wait to feel inspired before you implement a new behavior. You can immediately begin by gathering your willpower (a strong self-control determination that allows you to do something difficult) and stop procrastinating.

No doubt, you already know well how to schedule actions, including the ones you have been procrastinating about. The question is, what's holding you back from scheduling a time to start your action?

The key is to think about motivation as the desired outcome for completing a procrastinated action. In other words, motivation is the last step, not the first.

Asking yourself the following three questions may help you analyze your motivation in order to achieve a desired outcome:

• What is my main reason for completing the task?
• How will it make me feel when it's finally done?

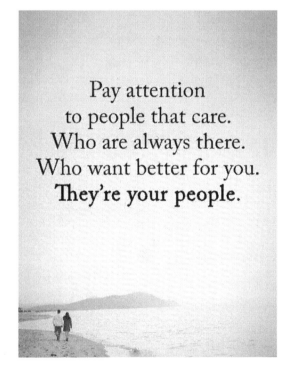

Pay attention
to people that care.
Who are always there.
Who want better for you.
They're your people.

Tip # 55

Own your greatness – say YES to your value, to serve, to receive money, to gaining clients. When we subconsciously believe that what we're offering has no value, we put that energy out and keep ourselves from receiving. Say YES to good things coming to you.

Tip # 56

Love – love yourself first, love what you are offering second, and love your audience enough to offer what your selling. Boom, lightbulb moment. A lightbulb moment is when you have an instance of mental and emotional clarity when your doubts vanish, and an illuminating truth is suddenly revealed. A light bulb moment is also an event when one suddenly understands something even if the concept had been explained several times before.

Tip # 57

There is no competition – everything is divinely inspired, which means just like there is an abundance of air and we don't worry about there not being enough air for us to breathe on this planet with billions of other people, there is an abundance of love, joy, success, and money for everyone.

Tip # 58

Flourish – let all that you are flourish; you weren't meant to work hard. So many of us are scared to flourish. We don't want to be any different in a world in which people are suffering. We often lie to ourselves and we discover, blending in is easy. Lots of people do it. Being your truest self can be the scariest thing in the world. Do everything from a place of love and let things happen rather than forcing them to happen.

Tip # 59

Expect it

Know it will happen and that everything will work out in your favor. Life will be a self-fulfilling prophecy to someone who doesn't believe. If you don't expect nothing, you won't receive anything. Get off your butt making excuses for why your broke and start going after things that will make you some money. God wants you to expect something out of life.

Tip # 60

Get out of debt

Create a plan to get out of debt now. You owe it to your future self to get out of debt now, so you don't have to worry about it later. How much student loan debt can you pay off this year? Do you still need to go back to school? You may still have a long way to go, but the journey of a thousand miles begins with a single step. After focusing on my own personal financial education, you must be committed to a plan to get out of debt and never get back into it. If you understand how much you get back every month by paying down your debt (which is exactly what you pay in interest), then getting out of debt becomes too good of a financial option not to do as a top priority.

It's so helpful to have someone guide you through how to create a budget that can help you understand why it's important to pay off debt — and how to do it asap.

Pay your future-self first

We've all heard the saying before that we should pay ourselves first, which means to put money into your savings account before spending on anything else.

However, it's equally important (if not more important) to pay your future-self as well by making long-term investments.

Looking for money for an upcoming wedding or a down payment on a home in the next year, that the stock market is not the place to be.

Instead, if you're in the market for the long haul, then time is on your side and the market will be up, which is generally the long-term trend.

However past performance does not guarantee future results but making a responsible long-term plan for your investments is a good idea, especially when you're in your 20s when you have lots of time.

YOU ARE NOT REQUIRED
TO SET YOURSELF ON
FIRE TO KEEP OTHER
PEOPLE WARM.

UNKNOWN

Tip # 61

Gratitude

We don't know if you know just how important Gratitude is. Our teacher taught us that the first commandment that Jesus gave was, **"to love God with all your heart, soul, mind and strength".** The beginning of recognition of all the wonderful things He has done, and continues to do, to enhance our lives. When you love God purely, your grateful. When you rise in the morning to see by His grace another day, your grateful. To look at His sun, you're grateful. You're grateful for the water that you use to refresh yourself after a night of sleep. You're grateful for the advancement in science that allows me these different tools that you use to make myself presentable. You're grateful for every insect, creature and flower and fruit and tree. Your grateful to be able to witness and marvel over His creation.

Gratefulness is love of God. So, when a teacher comes to give you what you didn't have, or shares with us knowledge, that you didn't have—that's from God. So, it is the love of God and the purity of heart that allows us to see Him everywhere we look and to be grateful for even a smile or a kind word.

Gracefulness aligns us with what we want, strengthens our expectations, brings us into the "miracle zone", and opens us up to receive more. Making daily gratitude lists is a powerful way to stay in alignment. It's impossible to feel 100% negative when you make note of everything, you're grateful for. Even if you can't think of much, the act of looking makes you feel better.

We should practice gratitude

Instead of throwing ourselves a pity party we should be grateful. A common idea is to write or name 3 things that you're grateful for every day. Record the good memories that are happening. Then when you're feeling cranky or can see a bad mood coming, you can open the list and get reminded of how much awesomeness is in your life.

Tip # 62

Welcome change

We can't receive new things if we stay in the same situations and patterns. Change isn't scary; it's bringing you closer and closer to your dream.

When a recent event such as a job loss, end of a relationship or illness has shaken you to the core, what do you do? Do you embrace the road you are now on or do you resist, react, and avoid change at all costs? It's a choice that will either paralyze you or propel you forward towards self-growth.

Being on the verge of impending change is probably one of the hardest places to be. At every fork in the road there are decisions that need to be made and questions about the outcome. The slate is blank and the only choices are to stay where you are or move forward.

What choice will you make? To get to the point of life-changing transformation, we need to do the work. And change, good or bad, is painful. It is the ending of one life and a beginning of another. How you do deal with that fear of the unknown? Do you jump into the next phase of your life allowing the "what if's" to consume your thoughts and dictate your actions? Or do you open yourself up to something different? Ask yourself how often you make unconscious decisions about your future that end up propelling you into self-sabotaging behavior?

You could turn the other cheek and continue doing what you've always done, or you could open your eyes to its gift. That gift is the opportunity you must create a conscious, healthy and wealthy life, the life that you really want.

Tip # 63

Visualize

This is another big one that people frequently mention to us. ed in almost every interview; the importance of visualizing your goals/dreams.

Everyone can use imagery to prepare for all kinds of situations, including public presentations and difficult interactions. Research has shown that surgeons, musicians, and business executives have used it to focus and to improve their performance. It could also help you run a 5K, ace a presentation, or even pass up the morning doughnut box.

Scientists believe that we may experience real-world and imaginary actions in similar ways. Whether we walk on a mountain trail or only picture it, we activate many of the same neural networks—paths of interconnected nerve cells that link what your body does to the brain impulses that control it. You can use this to your advantage in different ways. For example, imagining yourself doing movements can help you get better at them.

Mental workouts also stimulate the sympathetic nervous system, which governs our fight-or-flight response and causes increases in heart rate, breathing, and blood pressure. So simply envisioning a movement elicits nervous-system responses comparable to those recorded during physical execution of the same action.

Although it may sound like hocus-pocus, some research suggests that imagining could help you get results even when you don't move a muscle. Athletes who mentally practiced a hip-flexor exercise had strength gains that were almost as significant as those in people who actually did the exercise five times a week for 15 minutes on a weight machine.

If your challenge is more mental than physical—for instance, handling a difficult conversation—imagery can keep you calm and focused. Mentally rehearsing maintaining a steady assertiveness while the other person is ignoring or distracting you can help you attain your goal. Envisioning this calmness may also decrease physical symptoms of stress, like an increase in heart rate or stress hormones.

When you repeatedly imagine performing a task, you may also condition your neural pathways so that the action feels familiar when you go to perform it; it's as if you're carving a groove in your nervous system. Finally, on a purely psychological level, envisioning success can enhance motivation and confidence.

You must feel the dream, imagine already having it, engage every sense, step into the person/world you want to be in. When you've visualized correctly, you'll feel the shift, you'll feel excited!

Tip # 64

Do belief work

Everything that has happened to you has happened because you believed it was possible; this works for both bad and good things. If you have limiting beliefs as to what's possible for you, your dreams can't come to you. If you believe money is hard to make, that will be your experience. Sit down and write out your beliefs in an area you're having trouble in. If it's money, write down all your self-limiting beliefs on money. Realize them, write their opposite on the other side of the paper, rip the paper in half and burn or destroy the side with the bad beliefs. Release them and do this often, until they stop coming up as blocks for you.

Tip # 65

Surrender

State your intentions and goals, and then let go and allow for your dream or something even better to come to you.

I surrender

I am learning to live between effort and surrender.
I do my best and hope for what I want,
but I do not resist the direction of the wind.

Through surrender, I move from
outer turmoil to inner peace.
By letting go of expectations and outcomes,
I transform a painful experience
into a positive, fruitful endeavor.

When fear gets the best of me,
I surrender to love.
When I release my resistance to love's presence,
I am able to receive what I need —
what's trying to come into my life,
for my highest good.

Tip # 66

Look for clues

Look for clues that your dream is getting closer. This strengthens your expectation and keeps you excited. See everything as a positive sign. Did a friend recently achieve something you've been wanting? Their experience coming into your reality is a sign that your dream is coming closer! Look at it like the universe is asking me **"Is this what you meant? Is this what you want, too?"** Be happy for them, because when you are, you are telling the universe/God that you want the same thing!

Tip # 67

Doubt the doubt

Instead of doubting the dream, doubt any doubt that comes up for you. That's your inner critic feeling afraid.

Think of the last time you told yourself something critical or negative. Then think of the last compliment you gave yourself. Which is easier to remember?

Many of us—whether due to genetics, brain chemistry, our experiences or coping skills—tell ourselves way too many negative thoughts. We ruminate, thinking the same negative, unproductive thoughts over and over.

Be Aware

You need to know your thoughts to change them. Learn to notice when you are ruminating. Remind yourself that this is a waste of time. Write down the thoughts. Identify what triggered them. Be specific: **"My boss came in to talk to me and I started to worry that he hated my work and I am a loser."**

This brain dump clears your mind of the ruminative thoughts.

Tip # 68

Trust in perfect timing

It will happen. Don't give up and be grateful for all the lessons you've learned along the way to your dream.

Trust is the essence of relationships. You must practice taking responsibility for yourself and learning to listen to and trust your own being.

You must learn to trust your inner sense in shifting to questioning or observing. It involves trusting your intuition regarding the question to ask, feedback to give (with permission) and timing in doing either. Everything that happens is preparing you and stretching you to step into your dream.

Tip # 69

Blow the whistle on yourself– how are you not acting like the vision of yourself in your dream?

Are you stalling in life? Are you afraid to move forward? Do you have a proper vision of yourself? Do you even believe in your own message? What do you believe you deserve?

A lot of us doubt our deservingness.

Deservingness is not to be confused with entitlement. Entitlement is about believing you have a right to something. Deservingness is about how much you believe you're worth.

When you doubt your deservingness, what you're uncertain about is whether you measure up. Many of us carry around a secret shame that impacts our feelings of self-worth and deservingness. Our stories are individual, but our core experiences are very much the same. At some point in your life, someone told you there was something wrong with you. This is inevitable, of course, because there's something wrong with all of us.

It gets to dangerous and disempowering territory through repetition. If even one person in your life tells you repeatedly that there's something wrong with you, well, you can start to believe them.

Being rejected or criticized hurts, and it has a cumulative effect. Imagine every criticism you've ever received is a tiny little pin that landed right in your heart. Beyond hurting like hell, a heart full of pins holds you back and makes you play small. You are not small! We want you to stop acting like you are.

In life, you always create the results you believe you deserve. If you don't believe you deserve good things, you won't let yourself have them.

You'll sabotage, procrastinate, and excuse the good right out of your life if you don't believe you deserve it. Happily, you can raise your sense of deservingness, and deepen your feelings of personal worth. It's time to start believing in you again.

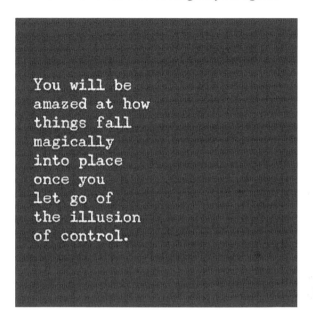

You will be
amazed at how
things fall
magically
into place
once you
let go of
the illusion
of control.

Tip # 70

Save for retirement

Start saving for retirement as soon as you can. There are so many ways to save for retirement, but a great place to start is with your employer's plan. If your employer offers a match, it's a good rule of thumb to invest up to the match at the least. If your budget allows you to save more, then save more (or up to the max). Saving for retirement early is important because you have the advantage of time that older people don't have.

It's not enough to simply start saving for retirement. You need to learn the basics of retirement saving.

You can start saving for retirement later

Right now, time is on your side. And by that, I mean, you can use the power of compound interest to your advantage. Allow us to put a little bit of math on you…

Let's assume that at age 30, Hakeema decides to invest $500 a month for 25 years. She then stops at age 55 and waits 10 years. At age 65, Dawn will have just over $800,000!

But Stephanika waited. At age 40, she decided to make the same investment and contribute $500 a month for 25 years. At age 65 she only has $407,000.

Do you see the power of compound interest? The same exact investment, but the one who started 10 years earlier ends up with almost DOUBLE the amount as the procrastinating investor. You cannot wait to start saving for retirement. It is making future you poor. Call Cecelia at 770-203-7111 and she can tell you how the rich are doing it so simply. Again – don't be intimidated.

Tip # 71

Stop thinking the day will be crap before it has even begun
You must make a conscious effort to be careful about how you speak to yourself when you wake up. If you think, **"Oh God, it's Monday"**, and you feel like crap before you even get out of bed, think of the effect on your body.

Whenever you recognize your feeling good or something good is happening, try sing or hum a few lines of a happy song. Use the same song every time (my song is Nina Simone's Feeling Good.) Then when I first wake up or I feel my mood starting to drop, I start singing my song in my head and I instantly feel better! Some sort of music/feeling/memory thingy (no idea the science behind it.) Sounds silly but it really works!

Tip # 72

Use your good stuff everyday
Pop open the Sparkling Apple Cider you got as a housewarming gift three years ago. Drink it out of a fancy glass.

Wear your diamonds, spritz your favorite perfume, burn your candles; stop saving your good stuff for a special day and make today a special day.

Tip # 73

Get enough Sleep

Sometimes you should go to bed early. After dishes are washed you can leave the laundry unwashed and completely ignore my to do list.

Most adults need 7 to 8 hours of good quality sleep on a regular schedule each night. Make changes to your routine if you can't find enough time to sleep.

Getting enough sleep isn't only about total hours of sleep. It's also important to get good quality sleep on a regular schedule so you feel rested when you wake up.

If you often have trouble sleeping – or if you often still feel tired after sleeping – talk with your doctor.

Try it. Change your sheets, take a hot shower, and celebrate going to sleep.

Tip # 74

Go out midweek

Now that you're getting a little more sleep you've got no excuses to stay out a little late. Make big plans for a Wednesday: go to a gig, meet up with friends and stay up too late, or catch a show. Just make sure you have coffee ready for the next morning and you're good to go.

Tip # 75

Do the hard jobs first

Do your hard jobs, the things you're dreading most on your to do list, first. We find that when you finally do something you've been avoiding, you get a little buzz – a mix of relief and a sense of accomplishment, that helps carry you through the day. Plus, once you're done your tough jobs, the rest of the day will seem easy.

Tip # 76

Watch the Sunset

When was the last time you watched the sunset? There is something magical about being outside at the golden hour, sipping on a cold drink and watching the sun slip below the horizon. But at home, this same magical hour is too often spent on the couch, looking at a screen.

The sun sets every day, so find some time each week to watch it and bring that 'on holiday' feeling to your day. Sunrise works too!

Tip # 77

Take your breaks

Sometimes we all lunch at our desks. But If you really struggle to get away for a proper break, at least get up from your desk more often. Make a coffee, walk to the printer, extra bonus points if you can go outside for a few minutes. While you're there look at the clouds and see how much better you feel about your Tuesday.

Tip # 78

Take steps to change your life

If you don't like your job, look for a new one. Don't be one of those people who tells people you hate your job and they are still paying you. If you can't make a big change now, start making baby steps. The sooner you start, the sooner you'll get to where you want to be. What do you need to do to prepare for a big change? Study? Pay off debt? Downsize?

Tip # 79

Create a special atmosphere at home
Even if you are just sitting on the couch, make it feel special. Burn incense or your favorite candles, get fresh flowers, or string up some lights. This should be much more romantic, right? Turn the TV off, put on some music, and chill out. You deserve it. You must not do anything at this time but enjoy it.

Tip # 80

Check your credit reports and your credit score annually
Check your credit reports and credit score annually for free using AnnualCreditReport.com. Not only will you be aware of your score, but you will know what is on your reports and whether there is any incorrect information listed. This is one way to know whether you've been a victim of identity theft.

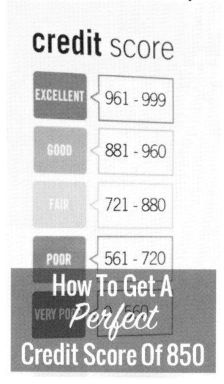

Tip # 81

Find a Passion Project
Create something that excites you – start scrapbooking, take up photography, learn to sew, start a small business, write – the possibilities are endless.
Do something that will get excited to get up and start working. Maybe you'll start sharing something that you've created with the world. Maybe it's constantly learning and trying to improve. It will give you a sense of satisfaction that you may struggle to find in your 'real' job.

Tip # 82

Stop counting down to the Weekend

Stop counting down to the weekend. When you're counting down, you're telling your brain today and everyday til Friday is crap and not worth living. Sometimes we turn on our cars and turn the radio on. You'll hear the radio broadcaster's voice "Hey everyone, I hope you all are having a wonderful morning. We are commercial free for two hours this morning! Thanks for listening to us on morning commute and remember, only two more days until Friday!" Now for us, we would hear that at 6:30 every morning with the only variation being the number of days, greater or smaller. Don't get us wrong. We love Fridays too, but within the past year or so, we've concluded that we need to live in the present. We need to make a personal and positive change in our lives. For the math-oriented folks: the average life expectancy in America is 78.84 years. Let's go crazy and give us 79 years. With 52 weeks in a year, there will be 52 Fridays, 52 Saturdays and 52 Sundays. Do the math, and that's 156 weekend days in a year, 12,324 in a lifetime. The Monday-Thursday stats are as follows: 2,018-week days in a year, 16,432 in a lifetime. You're telling me that you want to spend 57 percent of your days wishing it were another day of the week? Do that and you'll be unsuccessful in whatever you want to accomplish in life, not to our or anyone else's standards, but to your own. Only you know what drives you to wake up in the morning and go to work or school or wherever. You know what you want to accomplish in life and although it's very easy to unintentionally and quietly push that goal aside, it's unequivocally important to prevent yourself from doing that as well as to steer yourself back in the right direction if you do.
Be present and enjoy today.

Tip # 83

Resist the urge to complain

We know this is easier said than done, but we've learned that the quickest way to keep something from bothering you is to not complain about it. We know this goes against the popular belief that you should **"get things off your chest"** but in our experience, when you complain about something, it magnifies the situation. You draw attention to the issue and make it bigger than it needs to be.

Experience has taught us that complaining is a mindless habit. It's almost like a reflex and we do it without thinking—or, when we do it on purpose, it's usually a case of making lazy conversation. It's a tough habit to change but it's worth it. When we make the effort to stop complaining, we almost always feel better and hopefully, we even have a positive effect on the people around us. Take plenty and don't complain about it.

> When you complain, you make yourself a victim. Leave the situation, change the situation, or accept it. All else is madness.

Tip # 84

Look at the little picture
Sometimes we read too much into things, particularly when we are feeling rundown or tired or worse—hungry! When we're not feeling 100%, it's easy to misinterpret the intent behind other people's little comments or actions.

For example, **"I'm upset because someone ate the last cookie without offering me one"** morphs into **"I'm upset because no one here thinks about my feelings."** The truth is probably somewhere more along the lines of **"Everyone is just really, really hungry and likes cookies"** but sometimes reality is hard to see—and to be honest, it doesn't always matter.

Regardless of the real reason you missed out on a cookie, the truth is you can't control the things that happen to you, but you can control how you react. It's not always fair but the less you let things bother you, the happier you will be. This isn't to say you should never stick up for yourself but perhaps you should choose your battles, or at a minimum make sure there's actually a battle there to fight!

One quick and easy way to be less bothered is to focus on the little picture. When you feel yourself getting upset, pause for a moment; turn your attention to what's bothering you and try to frame it in its simplest form. For example:

… Instead of "The service in this restaurant is horrible!" (Outrage!)

Try "I'm upset because my waitress forgot to refill my coffee." (No big deal)

… Instead of "No one here respects my time."

(Sobs quietly at your desk)

Try "I'm upset because I asked a question in my email and he didn't answer it."

(Poor attention to detail, forgivable at 8 am on a Monday morning.)

Tip # 85

Choose Compassion + Focus on Humanity

If you find yourself getting upset with someone else—anyone from a loved one to a co-worker, you hardly know—you can fight feelings of annoyance by choosing compassion and focusing on their humanity.

Let's face it—it's very easy to get annoyed with people, but it's never a nice feeling. Sometimes you have a good reason and other times less so … but either way, letting go is often the best option and one easy way to do this is to think humanizing thoughts about the person who has upset you.

Even the person you are upset with has a story. Everyone does! We can use this knowledge to be more compassionate in our daily lives; next time you get annoyed with someone, try to shift your focus away from whatever did to upset you and instead, think of their stories.

If you don't know someone well, look for small details; think about how this person is always holding the door for you, or the way the lady ahead of you in the supermarket queue is speaking gently with her daughter. These little moments act as reminders that the person you're annoyed with is an actual person, with feelings and struggles just like you.

Tip # 86

Let go of expectations

Often, we have a picture of how we hope our day will play out in our minds. We imagine walking into our office early, making a nice hot cup of coffee, and having a fantastically productive morning. But, sometimes life happens: We can't find our keys and we're late out the door. Then, when we go to make our coffee … there's no milk. When we finally get to our desk and open our inbox, we are flooded with emails and when we next look up it's 10 am. Our morning is half over, we've had no coffee and we've done nothing on our to-do list.

At this point, it's easy to write the day off as a **"bad day"** because when we have high hopes for how things will turn out, it's disappointing when things don't go as planned. But the truth is our expectations are often clouding the reality of the situation.

If we can let go of our expectations and open our minds, we'll notice that yes, the day is off to a slow start, but it's far from over. There is still plenty of time to change course and turn things around.

Tip # 87

You dread the thought of cleaning surfaces or organizing papers (Or even organizing your thoughts)

Isn't it time you dusted the shelf in your bedroom? If the very thought of cleaning or organizing something is starting to make your stomach do summersaults, then you have too much on that surface or too much on your "plate". It should take just a couple of seconds to wipe down a surface or make a list of things to do today.

Tip # 88

Your considering moving homes or offices to fit your things in (or "feel more organized")

This is something a lot of us do without a second thought. But if you're looking to rent, lease, or buy an entirely new home or office just to store more of your items, or "start fresh" then this is really something of a worrying sign. You should be able to make the most of what you have.

Tip # 89

You have boxes under the bed, on your desk, or on the dresser

This doesn't sound like a big deal, but it has a big psychological impact on how big and spacious a room feels. It's important to include space in your home or office to let it breathe and this is a very important space that you should prioritize.

The same is true of your to-do list. If you're always pushing items to the bottom of the list, never being financially responsible like saving for emergencies or even a vacation, you'll never be able to truly go anywhere or on vacation with that feeling that everything is right with the world.

Tip # 90

Master your money mindset

What you believe about money is going to become your reality. When we didn't know anything about money, we felt broke and come at life from a complete scarcity view. Once we learned how to think differently about money everything changed. Here are some things we must do to master our money.

1.   **Change your money story**

For most of us, the story we tell ourselves about money is the root of all our issues.

2.   **Let go of money stress**

Money stress is common in life and in business. Put systems in place to end money stress once and for all.

3.   **Bust through your money blocks**

We all have them. Sometimes our negative self-talk or putting systems in place to reduce the stress can't completely clear them. These are further steps to take to be rid of the blocks preventing us from reaching our dreams.

4.   **Love your money**

Learning to love money is really the goal. Feel what it can do for you, your family and others. This feeling will help you from reverting back to negative feelings about money.

Tip # 91

Other good habits to start

As you start developing simple housecleaning and organization habits, you'll notice that your work will get easier and easier. This next set of tips will give you some great ideas for good habits to start

DELEGATE

Housework can be a huge job. Learn to delegate. Make chore charts for everyone in your house. Even small children can help pick up toys and other things. As you learn that you don't have to do it all, housework will become much easier.

FILL THE SINK WHEN YOU COOK

A good habit to start is filling your sink with hot soapy water every time you start to cook. This way you can **"clean as you go."** As you get done with each pot or dish, wash it quickly. This makes clean-up a snap.

SPRAY THE OVEN

Time for take-out? If there's a day when you're not using your oven, give it a quick spray of oven cleaner and forget about it. The next day, before you turn on your oven, give it a quick wipe down. You'll find that the baked-on stuff comes off much easier.

Tip # 92

Have a charity box

It's a good idea to keep a box or bag in your front closet that you put things you don't need anymore. This really helps get rid of clutter in your home. When the box is full, simply drop it off at your local Goodwill store.

Rinse your plate

This may be a small tip, but it can help in big ways. If you simply make it a habit to rinse your plate after dinner (and have all family members do the same), it will make washing them a lot easier. No one likes trying to wash dried food off dishes.

Tackle the small jobs

Housework can be overwhelming. Learn to break it down and tackle the smaller jobs first. As you do, each job will become easier. Also, if you clean the small messes before they get big, it'll be a lot easier to clean up.

Keep cleaner in the shower

A great shortcut for cleaning your tub and shower is to keep a bottle of shower cleaner handy. After you take a bath or shower, spray it down. You can take it a step further and keep a squeegee in it as well.

Tip # 93

Fast pick up before bed
If you make it a habit to do a quick pick up before going to bed, it'll really help. You'll find that it's easier to wake up and feel good about the day if even one room is clean.

Line your fridge
If you make it a habit to line your fridge shelves with paper towels, it'll make it a lot easier to clean. This will work especially well in the crispers, as the paper towels will soak up any extra wetness.

Take a trash bag with you
As you leave the house, make it a habit to take the trash out. This is a simple tip, but why make extra trips if you don't need to? This is also a great job to delegate to a teenager. They're always coming and going anyway.

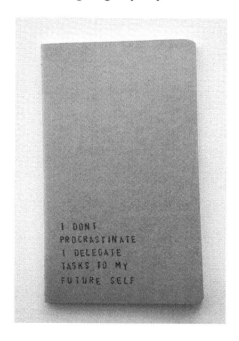

Tip # 94

How to stop procrastinating in 9 steps

Everyone does it, including you. You have things to do, important things or mundane things, and you put off doing them until the last minute. If Procrastination were an Olympic event you might be in the running for a gold medal, you're that good at it. You make jokes about being a world-class procrastinator with your friends, telling them that sure, you could finish that project right now if you wanted to but you're just going to do it tomorrow.

Procrastination is putting something off until later, either due to carelessness or habitual laziness. It's putting off until tomorrow what you just as easily could have finished up today. A procrastinator postpones or needlessly delays accomplishing something –just because.

A person who is habitually late to everything, from weddings to dates, is someone who procrastinates getting ready to leave. Maybe they don't start getting ready until it's nearly time to leave or they move so slowly that by the time they should leave for the event, they're still way behind schedule.

Why do you procrastinate anyways?

The behavior of procrastination affects almost everyone at one time or another in their life. For some, it is a continuous habit, part of who they are, a not-so-endearing character trait; for, others it may be a situational thing and doesn't affect too many events in their life. For whatever reason, people put off things they don't want to do.

Tip # 95

Because You Are Afraid.

No one likes to admit that they fear something, but fear might just be the reason you put off doing what you know you should do. Whether it's fear of failure or fear of success, it's still fear. Fear is a paralyzing and distressing emotion. It can stop us in our tracks-literally.

Because You Don't Think It's Important Enough

You don't place a high enough priority on the task at hand, it's not vital and so it's not worthy of you beginning it. You know the task needs to be done and you may already have decided that you're the one who must do it. However, there is always something else more important on your to-do list that keeps bumping that job back to the bottom.

You Don't Know Enough to do the Task

You may procrastinate beginning a project because you simply don't know everything you need to know in order to complete the task. You may not have consciously admitted this to yourself, but deep down you know it and it's coming out as an aversion to starting the project.

Because You're Too Busy

Life is busy. We have work and commitments and sometimes, we can't get to a task because we've run out of time in our busy day to complete one more thing.

Because It Works

Unfortunately, procrastination can reinforce itself. If we avoid something we don't want to do (like cleaning out the rain gutters) by engaging in behavior that we want to engage in (like hanging out with friends) then getting to it later, we can say that putting it off wasn't that bad after all. And besides, we had fun while we procrastinated.

You Haven't Committed to the Task at Hand

You may think the task should belong to someone else, it's not really your 'job' to do and the task is a waste of time. If this is how you're looking at this item, then you need to ask yourself what will happen to you if you don't complete it.

You Just Don't Want to Do It

Everyone is faced with jobs in life that they simply don't want to do. They're either gross, like having to clean toilets, or they're dangerous, like climbing up on the roof and cleaning the leaves out from the rain gutters. We put off doing the task at hand because we simply do not want to do it. Period. There is no underlying psychological reason for putting it off. It's that recalcitrant two-year-old in us coming out to say, **"I don't want to do it and I'm not going to"**.

You could just be lazy

Yes, that's what we said. We know it's not an easy thing to hear about yourself, but sometimes facing the truth about ourselves can help us overcome bad habits and succeed where we otherwise may have failed. You need to find a way to motivate yourself out of your habit of being lazy in order to stop procrastinating.

Tip # 96

How can you change your behavior and stop procrastinating?

Below are some strategies to help you stop procrastinating. Not every tip will work for every person, so take what you can from this list and see what works for you.

Take an inventory

Do you hear a little nagging voice in your head telling you that you need to do something? Can you see a visual in your head about the task you're avoiding and are you feeling the physical and emotional consequences of what will happen if you don't complete this task? Look for the clues that tell you just when and how you're procrastinating, and you'll be able to see that you are indeed putting something off.

Sometimes it's difficult to tell when you're procrastinating because you're attempting to avoid thinking about it but if you piece together the clues, you'll be able to pinpoint your behavior in order to get a handle on it.

Learn how you procrastinate

Do you think if you ignore the job at hand it will eventually go away and not bother you? Ignoring the problem/job won't cause it to disappear in a puff of smoke.

Do you over-estimate or under-estimate the degree of difficulty in completing the task? Do you scoff at the impact not finishing the task will have in your future? Perhaps you substitute something important for something important, like putting the dishes away instead of working on that term paper that's due in two hours. Maybe you take a short break but let that ''short' break turn into an all-night event, and therefore put off getting to that task you need to finish.

You might focus on one part of the job to the exclusion of the remaining task and thereby never finish the entire thing.

Once you recognize how you procrastinate, you'll better be able to put a stop to it. Often, we don't even realize that we are procrastinating until it's too late and we've missed a deadline.

Make yourself a productive environment

For example, if you work from home, create a home office where there's no TV to distract you from your work. Sure, that **"Walking Dead is on and it's Sunday night after all",** but you don't have time to watch it because you have a deadline for a client. If the TV is there, you'll be tempted to turn it on and then full-blown procrastination occurs. If you are addicted to the Internet but need to use your laptop or computer to do your work, then try to go somewhere where you won't be able to receive a signal and get online. Removing the temptation to do something other than what you need to do will help you put a stop to procrastination.

Tip # 97

Throw Out Those Procrastination Myths

"I work best under pressure". Once you believe that you can only work under pressure, you're giving yourself permission to procrastinate. This can snowball and create serious problems for you if you have several deadlines looming.

"I can't do this unless I have five uninterrupted hours" This is simply another stalling technique that master procrastinators use for telling themselves it's ok to not start the project because they won't have time to finish it. Hello? If you don't start the task, you'll never finish it. It's ok to start something and then stop so you can finish it later. Sometimes the simple act of beginning a task will break the cycle of procrastination and allow you to finish your job.

IS YOUR PROCRASTINATION A SIGN OF SOMETHING ELSE?

I can't do this unless it's perfect

The problem that most procrastinators have is that we are too hard on ourselves, demanding perfection where perfection is impossible. If you think you can't start your term paper until you have THE perfect opening sentence, then you have once again given yourself permission to put it off.

Break down the job

You have a job to do and it looks enormous. You could never, ever complete a job that big, so why even start? If that's your mindset, then you probably won't finish the job. In order to combat this kind of thinking, break the job or task down into small, manageable chunks. Your kitchen is a disaster, it's too much for you to handle. Start on one end and clean off one counter. Voila! You've started. Take baby steps and soon you'll see that the entire task has been completed.

Tip # 98

Change your attitude

Often we don't begin something we have to do because we tell ourselves how difficult it's going to be, or how disgusting the job is and how much we're going to hate doing it. By giving ourselves reverse-pep talks we give ourselves permission to avoid beginning the task at hand. When you hear yourself doing this, change your attitude. Be like the Little Engine that Could and tell yourself that you CAN do this, it's not that difficult. If you tell yourself that you don't know how to do a task, change that around to tell yourself that you can learn as you go. It's all a matter of mind over matter. If you think you can, you can.

Ask someone for help

It's true that you may not be able to do everything on your own. You're not Superwoman / Superman, though you do think you'd look cool in those red tights. It's not a sign of weakness to ask for help when you know that you can't do it on your own. If you don't understand a project, rather than putting it on the back burner (procrastinating), ask someone to clarify it for you. Once you understand it better, the fear of tackling it will be gone and you can proceed.

If you have a big job to do, then ask a friend to help you be accountable for working on it. Let them check up on you every so often to see that you're making progress and soon you'll find that the job is completed. The Buddy System works!

Keep what needs to be accomplished in plain sight

If you put away the project specs where you can't see them, it's much easier to not think about what needs to be done. Leave your work where you can see it, as a visual reminder of what you must do. If it's hidden, it's forgotten.

Learn how to tell time

You already know how to tell time and you can even do it on a clock without a digital readout. But did you know that world-class procrastinators have unrealistic views of the time it takes to accomplish something? It's true. You'll tell yourself that a certain task will only take three hours to complete, so you really don't have to start it right this minute. You can wait till later and then you'll finish it up in three hours. What you fail to realize is that other things can happen along the way to distract you and stretch that three hours into six and soon you've missed that deadline. Starting now is a good best option.

Keep Yourself on a Schedule

Take a calendar and write down all the things that you must do, the blocks of time that are taken up with things already scheduled. The blank spaces in between those times are the times when you can work on your task. Make sure you don't over-schedule your time and under-estimate the time you'll need to finish a project.

Set a time limit

Maybe the task at hand is something you really don't want to do. That happens to all of us and there's no shame in admitting that you would simply rather not do it. However, if it's a job that you must do, here's a good tip on how to not procrastinate. Tell yourself that you're going to work on it for one hour. Devote that one hour to the project or task and then stop. Set another time limit the following day, depending upon when the job needs to be accomplished.

Knowing that you don't have to do something unpleasant all right now will go a long way towards helping you avoid not doing it at all.

Make a List. Make a list for everything. Make a list for the things you are going to accomplish each day, and even a list of the lists you need to make. Making a list can also be a useful tool in helping you avoid procrastinating. down a list of what you need to accomplish.

Put it in order of importance, highest to lowest. Next, start with number one and work your way down the list, checking off items as you go. Not only will this help you be organized but putting those little check marks next to items you've finished will give you a mental boost and help you feel successful. And who doesn't like to feel successful?

Basic human nature will always play a role in procrastination. Pleasurable activities are infinitely more enticing than painful or dull ones. Consciously determining why, you procrastinate will go a long way in helping you change your behavior. Don't expect to transform your habits overnight but do take small steps in the right direction and you'll eventually get there. If you reward yourself for your little successes in this area, you just might make non-procrastination more pleasurable than full-blown-avoidance-procrastination.

14 Daily Practices to
OVERCOME PROCRASTINATION
or How to Get Rid of Your Laziness

1 **Resolve Any Potential Emergency**
Taking care of emergencies immediately will prevent scarier issues down the road.

2 **Do a 5- to 10-Minute Daily Review**
Spend a few minutes going over the day's priorities.

3 **Focus On Your MITs**
Identify the tasks that have the biggest impact on your life and do them first.

4 **Eat the Frog**
If you can complete the hardest task first, all other tasks will seem less daunting.

5 **Use the Eisenhower Matrix**
The Eisenhower Matrix prioritizes your tasks by urgency and importance.

6 **Complete Quick Tasks Immediately**
If you know a task takes only a few minutes, then do it right away.

7 **Create a Mini Habit for Challenging Tasks**
Set a "lowball" goal that makes it super simple to get started.

8 **Build Elephant Habits for Ongoing Projects**
Chip away at a simple but time-consuming project in 5- to 15-minute daily increments.

9 **Use Sprints to Work On Challenging Projects**
Work for a short period of time and then give yourself frequent breaks.

10 **Build the Discomfort Habit**
Discomfort is not a bad thing and a little discomfort is healthy.

11 **Build the Awareness Habit**
Create a habit where you track your impulses to procrastinate.

12 **Bundle Rewards with Actions**
Engage in a specific enjoyable experience only while you're engaging in an activity that has a positive long-term impact on your life.

13 **Attach All Tasks to a Goal**
"How does this relate to one of my important goals?"

14 **Create Accountability for Your Tasks**
When you have someone to cheer on your successes, you're less likely to give up.

Tip # 99

Clear your mind

One of the reasons you're in a bit of a slump is because you've got too much going on in that wonderful brain of yours?

You need to take a moment to step outside of yourself and clear your mind of all the noise.

We can't stress the importance of this first step enough. You're not going to be able to get out of your slump unless you have a thorough detox of all your negative thoughts holding you back!

Also, once you start trying to fill your head with ideas, you may not be able to stop - so we need to have a little clear out first!

Here are ways you can clear your mind and get inspired:
take a moment to be by yourself and just breathe

- go for a long walk in nature - leave your headphones at home!
- take a bath with candles, calming music and LOTS of bubbles
- sit in silence - this helps us just be at peace and stay calm, but it might not work for everybody!
- watch an old favorite - watch something you've seen again and again so you don't really need to concentrate.

It doesn't matter how you do it, if you are taking the time to get your mind clear of obstacles.

As someone who is constantly stressing and worrying, you may find this super useful. It's nice to be alone and think things through at our own pace.

Once you've cleared your mind, come back to your workspace and grab a pen and paper. Write down some thoughts you had whilst you took time to yourself. Did you have any realizations or ideas - business or personal?

Tip # 100

Have some 'you' time
Question: How do you get out of a slump without some time to do your own thang?
Answer: You don't.

We live in a world where it is incredibly easy to access some good old forms of escapism and hit 'snooze' on reality. We mean, we don't know about you, but I could watch our favorite shows on television all night.

Remember that after all the hustle and bustle, you still need to make sure you're keeping Number 1 happy. Read a book. Watch some Netflix. Dance like nobody's watching!

Do what you love most (and often) or you'll find yourself overworked and overwhelmed. Nobody wants that!

Think of 3 things that make you happy (like deep down, warm and fuzzy, happy). Try to do at least one of those things a week.

Tip # 101

Focus on building assets

Assets increase your net worth and are the key to building wealth. Wealthy people have assets. If you want to build wealth, get out of debt and acquire assets. You'll watch your net worth grow, and you'll be amazed at how you can change your financial future just by adhering to simple rules.

Tip # 102

Not anticipating the tough times.

Whether you want to get out of debt, or you're hoping to lose weight, change isn't easy. You'll encounter some days that are harder than others and it's important to accept that there will be a rough road ahead. Think about potential pitfalls that you might face and develop a plan for dealing with those times when you might be tempted to give up. When you have a plan, you'll feel more confident in your ability to keep going.

Tip # 103

29 WAYS TO STAY CREATIVE

1 MAKE LISTS

2 CARRY A NOTEBOOK EVERYWHERE

3 TRY FREE WRITING

4 GET AWAY FROM THE COMPUTER

5 QUIT BEATING YOURSELF UP

6 TAKE BREAKS

7 SING IN THE SHOWER

8 DRINK COFFEE

9 LISTEN TO NEW MUSIC

10 BE OPEN

12 GET FEEDBACK

13 COLLABORATE

11 SURROUND YOURSELF WITH CREATIVE PEOPLE

14 DON'T GIVE UP DON'T GIVE UP DON'T GIVE UP DON'T GIVE UP DON'T GIVE UP DON'T GIVE UP DON'T GIVE UP DON'T GIVE UP DON'T GIVE UP DON'T GIVE UP DON'T GIVE UP DON'T GIVE UP

15 PRACTICE, PRACTICE, PRACTICE

16 ALLOW YOURSELF TO MAKE MISTAKES

17 DO SOMETHING NEW

18 COUNT YOUR BLESSINGS

19 GET LOTS OF REST

20 TAKE RISKS

21 BREAK THE RULES

22 DON'T FORCE IT

23 READ A PAGE OF THE DICTIONARY

24 CREATE A FRAMEWORK

25 STOP TRYING TO BE SOMEONE ELSE'S PERFECT

26 GOT AN IDEA? WRITE IT DOWN

27 CLEAN YOUR WORK PLACE

28 HAVE FUN

29 FINISH SOMETHING

Tip # 104

Know that mental healthcare isn't one-size-fits-all
I was once told ... 50% of success comes from good medications, but you cannot rely on meds alone. The other 50% comes from the mental effort and positive thinking you must do every day, whether is it is going to counseling or being an active leader of your life choices and thoughts. You cannot succeed by sitting in the backseat and just taking meds. You must put in mental effort every day to gain success and be mentally healthy.

Tip # 105

Let people help you
Know that even though people may not understand you, the ones who love you will try to help you as much as they can. Trust them and rely on them, you don't have to handle it all alone. So many of us hate the thought that we might need help in our lives. We believe the being independent is sexy! Right?
Independence looks impressive on the surface – but it has a sinister shadow.
What's lurking in the shadow? Fear. Of being hurt; of appearing 'needy'; of reaching out only to be rejected.
We stall our personal growth, business endeavors and relationships (all of which thrive on interdependence, delegation and intimacy). You could even say independence is at the root of humanity-wide level catastrophe.
Yes, independence is as inauthentic as its more well-known and mocked opposite, co-dependence. And they are equally damaging. How do we know when dependence levels are healthy, and we have attained that holy grail of all things – balance?
How about when we are able to allow ourselves be supported without feeling excessively vulnerable? When we can care for someone from a place of wholeness, and not because we need that in order to feel whole?

Below are some approaches to dealing with yourself from both sides of the spectrum.

Attributes Of The Dysfunctionally Independent (DIP)

How do you know when you are being dysfunctional independent?
You are too proud, afraid, and/or anal to accept help.
You never let anyone give to you. Intimacy is unfamiliar and frightening.
You suffer from 'here I go again on my own' syndrome (and you're proud of it).

You appear cool, but you know you are just cut off from your feelings.

You feel lonely.

You are afraid of commitment.

Your attempts at healing are solitary.

You prefer your dog's company to other people.

Dysfunctional Independence + Embracing Reliance = Interdependence

Realizing that we are DIPpy isn't just something new to make ourselves wrong for. It just means integrating the aspects of us that we have shut down because we previously made it wrong!
For the dysfunctionally independent, that is neediness. For the codependent, that is worthiness/power).
We start by reliving our old wounds.
Key questions to ask yourself: when did you decide to become so independent? Who hurt you? Who let you down? Go to town in reflecting on your childhood.
Also, be open to some externally sourced help and insight with this (from a therapist or a coach).
The good news is that anytime we reclaim aspects of ourselves that we have disowned, we get our energy and creativity back.

Other good practices for recovering DIPs:

Notice when you are judgmental of people that you perceive as being 'needy'. If it provokes a strong reaction in you, it means you are likely projecting. Love and accept the part of you that feels needy sometimes too. Or as a close friend of mine says – 'own that stuff'.

Say to yourself, 'today I will receive'. Ask yourself, 'who could I be asking for help from?'

Look around you and notice how supported you are being all the time. (The barista that made you your morning coffee. The workpeople that made the road safe for you to drive on).

Truthfully, the notion of independence is a fallacy: if we're alive, we need help.

Tip # 106

And teach them how to do it.
It's OK to ask for help and it is beneficial to tell people exactly how you need them to comfort you (hug me, listen to me, offer advice). In the moment it's easy to worry that their comfort won't mean as much because you've told them what to do, but it is so awesome to be comforted in the way you need, and most people are willing to do exactly what you ask for. It also makes them more willing to help you in the future because they know what to do.

Tip # 107

Learn to tell when the voice in your head belongs to your depression
Sometimes the best thing that we can do to help ourselves is to separate which thoughts are mine and which belong to anxiety or depression. For example, you might get the thought: **"Why bother going to the club meeting? No one wants me there anyway."** The first thing you should do is attribute the thought to depression. It is not an organic thought of yours; it is depression mimicking your voice and whispering in your ear. This helps you to separate yourself from any negative emotions the thought might give you.

Tip # 108

Don't let other people's chaos become your chaos
A person who works in the mental health field gave us this advice.
We use this at work and in our personal life to give ourselves
permission to let go of drama and other exhausting and non-essential
"emergencies" from other people.

Tip # 109

Use apps to cope with anxiety
We hope you don't suffer from anxiety attacks. When you begin to
feel overwhelmed use the app **ReachOut Breathe**, and it will give
you something to focus on while also talking you through some
breathing exercises.

Tip # 110

Allow yourself to feel your feelings
Sometimes you must simply feel what you are feeling; to not cover it
up or try to be strong, but to just allow yourself to feel. Even if it
hurt, even if you didn't want to face it, but to just let it happen. It's a
very natural and therapeutic way to cope with mental health issues,
or simply anything difficult that comes your way. Allow yourself to
feel.

Tip # 111
Just say "no" if you really need to

Sometimes it's OK to retreat to your bed and hide under your bed.
You can fight long and hard to function in the world so it's ok to take
a break. Also, it's OK to say no every now and again. If you are
finding that you have been coping with social situations a lot, then
you will need time to recharge your batteries.

Tip # 112

SELF-AWARENESS, SELF-ACCEPTANCE, AND TRUST IN YOUR INNER CAPACITIES ARE ESSENTIAL TO RESILIENCE. THESE CAPACITIES CREATE A HOME BASE, A SECURE SENSE OF SELF FROM WHICH YOU CAN RESPOND FLEXIBLY TO ALL OF LIFE'S DIFFICULTIES. WHEN YOU TURN YOUR FOCUS INWARD, YOU FEEL SAFE, AT HOME, AND AT PEACE.

Tip # 113

Think of yourself as an ant

After you have said something wrong in a social situation or when you mess up at work think of yourself as an ant. You are just an ant, no one cares, the world has not changed because of your one mistake. It helps. Realizing that on this giant earth with billions of people, you're just a single person, like an ant on a sidewalk should give you great relief.

Tip # 114

Comfort yourself the way you would comfort a friend
We always find it helpful to think of things from a third person perspective. So, if a friend was feeling stupid or worthless, you wouldn't say **"Yeah, you are pretty stupid and worthless".** You would say the opposite. We are often way harsher with ourselves than we are with others.

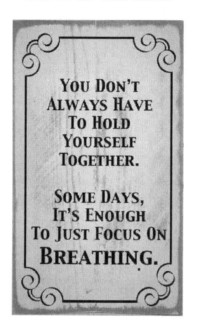

YOU DON'T
ALWAYS HAVE
TO HOLD
YOURSELF
TOGETHER.

SOME DAYS,
IT'S ENOUGH
TO JUST FOCUS ON
BREATHING.

Celebrate small victories because they add up
We have a perspective on celebrating and reaching for small
victories. If you keep climbing small rocks, you'll eventually
conquer the mountain. You must physically make a point to
celebrate small victories on my journey because you realize more
and more just how important it is. When we deflect giving ourselves
credit for finally accomplishing something, no matter how small and
insignificant it seems, our motivation and hope vanishes.
When we fail to acknowledge and celebrate small victories, we get
discouraged and the flame inside us starts to dwindle.
Unfortunately, taking the time to celebrate small victories is
basically frowned upon in society. It's almost as if we're not allowed
to get excited about anything. How dare you belly laugh in public?
Don't even think twice about shrieking in elation when you see your
long-lost pal walk through the door.
WHY ARE WE LIKE THIS? Why are we ashamed or afraid to feel
joy and express that joy…and why do we make other people feel
confined to exactly 0 emotions?

**Separate the things that are stressing you out and put them in
their own compartments**
A counselor once told us to compartmentalize: Draw a grid with
several boxes and list your stressors or reason for anxiety in each
box. Separating stress from school, work, relationships, etc. in a
tangible way can help the overwhelming feeling of processing them
all in your mind at once. Go through each box on the grid and list
ways you can make the situation better, or facts that prove the issue
is not worth feeling anxious about. Tackling each point of stress one
at a time on paper calms me down and helps me feel more in control.

Tip # 117

Get through just 10 seconds at a time

For example, you may have to serve food at a restaurant. You sometimes feel like you screw up with every one of your tables at once and it seems like the world is ending. In the heat of the moment you must remind yourself that this feeling, and these tables, will get up and leave and this stress will be totally over. You just must get through it 10 seconds at a time until it does.

Tip # 118

Meditate

Meditate for just five to 10 minutes a day, and you'll see a remarkable change in your willpower. Meditation can also help you better snap out of your cravings and bring you back to reality. And don't worry if you're having trouble meditating and focusing. Being "bad" at meditation is actually good for self-control. You'll be more focused after practicing, because you'll be able to better catch yourself moving away from the goal and recognize your impulses.

Tip # 119

Relax

Relaxing will help ease stress and anxiety, which in turn boosts your willpower reserve. You might think that's easy and start kicking back with your favorite TV show or a big meal. However, true relaxation, according to the book, is giving your body and mind a break to trigger the physiological relaxation response. In a relaxed state, your heart rate and breathing slow down, blood pressure drops, muscles release tension, and more.
We recommend lying in bed, close your eyes, and take deep breaths. If your body is tense, she suggests flexing the muscle in the affected parts of your body and letting it go. Studies show that people who practice daily relaxation exercises have healthier physiological responses to stressful willpower challenges.

Tip # 120

Just because the
past didn't turn
out like you wanted
it to, doesn't mean
your future can't
be better than you
ever imagined.

Tip # 121

Somewhere in your life, there's going to be a point where you have a
decision to make. You're going to have to choose between taking the
easy route and the hard route. A lot of people take the easy route and
they have a good life that way. But the better life was by taking the
hard route. You may have 20 years of pain and suffering to try and
get past it, but a lot of us die before truly starting our journey. Don't
die before you start your journey.

Tip # 122

Stop Feeling Sorry for Yourself

It's not going to help the situation. It'll only help you to wallow in a state of apathy, playing the victim. The kind of person that things happen to, but that can't do anything about it. By stopping feeling sorry for yourself, you can get on and DO something about it. If you want to be happy – stop feeling sorry for yourself. Self-pity is our worst enemy and if we yield to it, we can never do anything wise in this world.

Tip # 123

Remember that no one is judging you as much as you are.
No one is ever thinking about you as much as you believe they are, because everyone is too busy worrying about themselves. Take care of you, and not the you that you feel you're perceived as.

Tip # 124

Make small deadlines

Researchers found that if participants control one small thing that they aren't used to controlling, it helps to train and strengthen the willpower muscle. You can do this by setting small deadlines and trying to tackle a task piecemeal. For example, if your goal is to eat healthy, you can set a mini goal of just browsing the produce aisle in the supermarket in the first week, then resolve to cook one healthy meal for the second week.
Keep setting these small deadlines for a few months, and without realizing it, you'll accomplish what you set out to do. The consistent act of self-control can increase overall willpower.

Tip # 125

Remember the reasoning

Before you give in to your impulse, try to remember why you resolved not to do it in the first place. Think of your long-term goals and compare them to the short-term satisfaction you get from caving into temptation. You'll then realize that the "treat" is now a threat and an obstacle to your goals.

Tip # 126

Be supportive of yourself, not critical

There's nothing that drains willpower faster than guilt and shame. So, don't try to incentivize yourself by beating yourself up over your failures. Focus on what you can do instead of what you should not do. For example, resolve to eat more healthy meals instead of restricting desserts. If you berate yourself, you could trigger the **"what-the-hell"** effect, which basically derails you from your goal after a mistake and makes you more susceptible to temptation.

Tip # 127
Pre-commit

Make it inconvenient to give in to your temptation. It won't stop you, but it will make it harder to go against your goals. For example, schedule a session with a personal trainer or bring a set amount of cash with you when you're on a budget and leave your credit cards at home.

Tip # 128

Associate with your future self

We often put off tasks we don't want to do and tell ourselves that we'll get it done later. However, "later" seems to get postponed to the point where it sometimes doesn't happen. This may happen because you are disconnected with your future self. Brain-imaging studies show that we even use different regions of the brain to think about our present selves and our future selves. The brain has a habit of treating your future self like a stranger, which can affect your current efforts to reach long-term goals.

Think about it this way: you seem to assume that your future self will get everything done and is a superhuman who can do it all. You may be indulging in treats now, but you're letting your future self-suffer the consequences. Don't treat your future self poorly; work to associate your current state to your future self. If you visualize your future, your brain will start to think more rationally about your current choices. Imagine yourself working out if your aim is to get fit. Another strategy that works is to write a letter or an email to your future self. Write about your hopes for the future, what you think you will be like, and what your future self will say about your current choices.

Tip # 129

Move on without them

If you know someone who insists on destructively dictating the emotional atmosphere, then be clear: they are toxic. If you are suffering because of their attitude, and your compassion, patience, advice, and general attentiveness doesn't seem to help them, and they don't seem to care one bit, then ask yourself, **"Do I need this person in my life?"**
When you delete toxic people from your environment it becomes a lot easier to breathe. If the circumstances warrant it, leave these people behind and move on when you must. Seriously, be strong and know when enough is enough! Letting go of toxic people doesn't mean you hate them, or that you wish them harm; it simply means you care about your own well-being.

A healthy relationship is reciprocal; it should be giving and taking, but not in the sense that you're always giving and they're always taking.

Tip # 130

Stop pretending their toxic behavior is OK
If you're not careful, toxic people can use their moody behavior to get preferential treatment, because it just seems easier to quiet them down than to listen to their grouchy rhetoric. Don't be fooled. Short-term ease equals long-term pain for you in a situation like this. Toxic people don't change if they are being rewarded for not changing. Decide this minute not to be influenced by their behavior. Stop tiptoeing around them or making special pardons for their continued belligerence.
Constant drama and negativity is never worth putting up with. If someone over the age 21 can't be a reasonable, reliable adult on a regular basis, it's time to speak up about it.

Tip # 131

Speak up and stand up for yourself!
Some people will do anything for their own personal gain at the expense of others – cut in line, take money and property, bully and belittle, pass guilt, etc. Do not accept this behavior. Most of these people know they're doing the wrong thing and will back down surprisingly quickly when confronted. In most social settings people tend to keep quiet until one person speaks up, so SPEAK UP.
Some toxic people may use anger as a way of influencing you, or they may not respond to you when you're trying to communicate or interrupt you and suddenly start speaking negatively about something dear to you. If ever you dare to speak up and respond adversely to their moody behavior, they may be surprised, or even outraged, that you've trespassed onto their behavioral territory. But you must speak up anyway.

Not mentioning someone's toxic behavior can become the principal reason for being sucked into their mind games. Challenging this kind of behavior upfront, on the other hand, will sometimes get them to realize the negative impact of their behavior. For instance, you might say:

"I've noticed you seem angry. Is something upsetting you?"
"I think you look bored. Do you think what I'm saying is unimportant?"
"Your attitude is upsetting me right now. Is this what you want?"

Direct statements like these can be disarming if someone truly does use their moody attitude as a means of social manipulation, and these statements can also open a door of opportunity for you to try to help them if they are genuinely facing a serious problem.

Even if they say: **"What do you mean?"** and deny it, at least you've made them aware that their attitude has become a known issue to someone else, rather than just a personal tool they can use to manipulate others whenever they want.

Tip # 132

Put your foot down

Your dignity may be attacked, ravaged and disgracefully mocked, but it can never be taken away unless you willingly surrender it. It's all about finding the strength to defend your boundaries.

Demonstrate that you won't be insulted or belittled. To be honest, you may have never had much luck trying to call truly toxic people out when they've continuously insulted you. The best response you've received is a snarky, **"I'm sorry you took what I said so personally."** Much more effective has been ending conversations with sickening sweetness or just plain abruptness. The message is clear: There is no reward for subtle digs and no games will be played at your end.

Truly toxic people will pollute everyone around them, including you if you allow them. If you've tried reasoning with them and they aren't budging, don't hesitate to vacate their space and ignore them until they do.

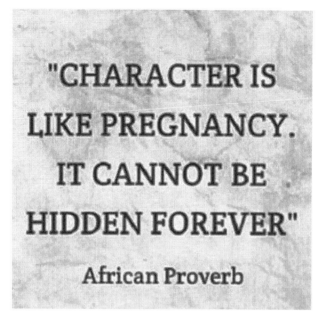

"CHARACTER IS LIKE PREGNANCY. IT CANNOT BE HIDDEN FOREVER"
African Proverb

Tip # 134

Know that you can't change a situation by worrying
Overthinking something you can't do anything about can't change the outcome anyway, so it's of no use.
Oftentimes, when people get in their heads, they get into trouble. A recent study of more than 30,000 people showed that focusing on negative events (particularly through rumination and self-blame) can be the biggest predictor of some of today's most common mental health problems.
Time spent alone in thought can be positive – a rich environment for personal growth and creativity. Yet, getting **'in our heads'** can also be dangerous when we are negatively turned against ourselves.
There is an important difference between introspection and rumination. While introspection involves healthy self-reflection and exploration, rumination is more like a vicious cycle of negative thinking and critical, demoralizing self-talk. While introspection can lead to self-understanding, insights, solutions and goal-setting, rumination can make us feel self-critical, self-doubting, stifled or even self-destructive.

Much of the time, when we are overthinking, we are engaging in a destructive thought process that leads to unfavourable outcomes. We are listening to a critical inner voice in our heads that hones in on the negative aspects of a situation. This voice is like a sadistic coach that feeds us a ceaseless stream of criticism and undermines our goals. It's that thought that pops up when we are about to go on a job interview: **"You'll never get this. You're going to embarrass yourself. Just look how nervous you are."** It's the dialogue that plays in your head analysing your relationship: **"Why is she so distant today? I must have said something stupid. She's losing interest. She probably likes someone else."**

Take note of what the critical inner voice is telling you and when it comes up.
At those times when you notice yourself overthinking, it's helpful to verbalize what that destructive coach in your head is telling you. Are you having mean thoughts toward yourself, attacking your performance at work? **"You sounded so stupid in the meeting today. Everyone thinks you don't know what you're doing now. You're incompetent! Just keep your head down and maybe no one will notice you."** The coach may also be tricky and come across as self-soothing. **"You should relax. You don't have to get to that project tonight. You deserve a break. Just settle down."** Of course, that same soothing-sounding voice can turn on a dime and beat you up for not achieving your goals. **"You're so lazy. Look at you just lounging around all night. You never finish anything."** Both self-attacking and self-soothing voices lead you to the same undesirable outcome. That is why it is so important to catch on to these thoughts. Notice when they arise and what specifically they're telling you.

Tip #135

Think About Where These Voices Come From
When you become aware of the specific thoughts you have toward yourself or others, you may start to see a pattern. Do you often feel more critical of your spouse when he or she brings up a certain subject? Do you turn on yourself when you're talking to your children, your parents, your boss, a sibling or your partner? Once you come to know the types of critical inner voices you're experiencing, you can think about the real source of these thoughts.

You may be surprised to learn they have very little to do with you and your real feelings in your current life or in the current situation.

For example, did someone treat you like you were stupid or incapable as a child? Were you taught to fend for yourself or not to trust others? All kinds of attitudes your parents or important early caretakers had toward themselves and toward you can seep into your consciousness and manifest themselves as your critical inner voice.

Understanding where these attitudes come from can help you to separate them from your real point of view, while having more compassion for yourself.

Tip # 136

Don't always listen to the voice in your head - Stand Up to Your Critical Inner Voice

Journaling is a very helpful way to track what your critical inner voice is telling you. One very helpful exercise is to write down these **"voices"** or thoughts as **"You"** statements instead of **"I"** statements. i.e. **"You're so ugly"** as opposed to **"I'm so ugly." "I'm useless; I always mess up"** becomes **"you're useless; you always mess up."**

This small-seeming alteration helps you to view the voice as an enemy and to see where it may have originated from in your past. It also paves the way for you to then respond to these voices from a more realistic and compassionate perspective.

We recommend that you write down or verbalize a reply to each of these thoughts the way a friend would talk to you, i.e. **"I'm an attractive person with a lot to offer." "I'm valuable and competent in many ways."** The idea of this exercise isn't to boost your ego. It really is about taking on a more honest and kinder attitude toward yourself, the sort of attitude you'd have toward a good friend.

As you come to know your inner critic, you can see how listening to it can influence your behavior. Pay attention to how your critical inner voice perpetuates that cycle of overthinking. Notice when it tells you to do harmful things like, **"Just isolate yourself. Have that third piece of cake. Don't tell her how you feel. Keep him at a distance."** Then, make a conscious effort to act on your REAL point of view and go for what you want. Although the voice may get louder at first, like an angry toddler throwing a tantrum, eventually it will quiet down, as your real self is strengthened. Just because you had a cripplingly negative thought about yourself doesn't mean it's true.

Tip # 137

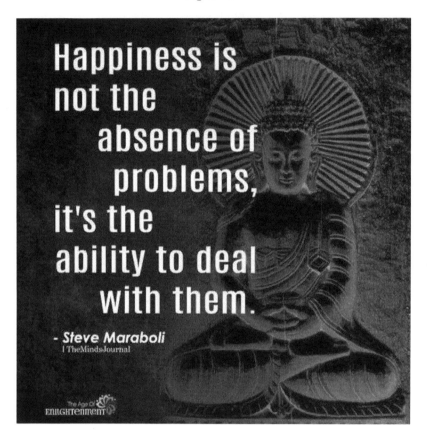

Happiness is not the absence of problems, it's the ability to deal with them.

- *Steve Maraboli*
I TheMindsJournal

The Age Of
ENLIGHTENMENT

Tip # 138

Know that you deserve to get help
Perhaps you believe, Mental health issues aren't really that bad and that has very much affected how and when we seek treatment. Our therapists are right when they tell us that no matter how mild or how severe, our depression matters, and it deserves to get treated. We deserve to get help, and that changes how we view our mental health entirely.

Tip # 139

Don't feel ashamed or weak for needing medication
If we were diabetic, would we think ourselves weak for using insulin? Of course not. If you need psychiatric medication, it is for a very real medical condition that just happens to be in your brain, not your pancreas. Don't feel ashamed or weak or guilty, just do what you need to keep yourself healthy.

Tip # 140

Don't stop your medication without talking to your doctor
Take your meds. We often think that this muted version of ourselves is too boring and want to go off our medication. It always starts out great. We have more ideas and motivation, but after a few days to weeks it turns to racing thoughts that just can't stop and our mind starts interpreting things wrong, and we get paranoid and start hearing voices confirming our paranoid delusions. We end up in the mental hospital and must go back on the meds anyway. So, we have to remember, just take the meds.

Tip # 141

Track data to help you identify patterns in how you're feeling day to day
We should track ourselves: sleep, food, mood, activity, medications, physical complaints, and significant events. It helps us see connections between our mental state and other variables in our life, which lets us make choices that are better for our mental health or identify the impact of changes.

Tip # 142

Don't assume you have to fix everything yourself
If something is wrong, admit that something is wrong, and decide that you're going to fix it. You don't have to know what to call the problem, or know the solution, but decide that you're going to work to get better.

Tip # 143

Strive for happiness, not for perfection
When we were first experiencing severe depression as a teenager, we confided in a friend's mom, who said to us, **"Work to be happy, not perfect."** We're still fighting depression to this day, but those words have stuck with us for the past ten years.

Tip # 144

8 THINGS THAT CHANGE YOUR LIFE IN ONE YEAR

1. Stop complaining and appreciate how lucky you are every day.
2. Embrace loneliness and reinvent yourself in the process.
3. Say goodbye to the people that don't bring positive energy into your life.
4. Throw off the TV and set Internet controls.
5. Pick one skill you want to cultivate and put all your effort into developing it.
6. Commit to the goals you set and never look back.
7. Sweat every day to boost your mood.
8. Fail forward. Learn from every mistake you make.

ART
OF THE
INITIATE

Tip # 145

There's no point in budgeting when you don't make much money

We believed this lie for way too long. Having barely enough money to pay bills and feed our family (sometimes not enough), what is the point in budgeting?

If you don't get a plan for your money, then you will never get out of that situation. Not budgeting – even when you are in dire financial straits – is a recipe for perpetual poverty.

Here's one reason why – when your income does eventually increase, you will be so used to having no income leftover that your spending will simply increase accordingly, and you won't even realize it. And you will remain broke.

Tip # 146

You can't invest

Investing simply means taking some of what you have now, and instead of consuming it, putting it to use to make your future better. That's it. It doesn't mean that you must hire a broker and watch the stock ticker on CNBC all day long.

This could be investing in an IRA, investing in your children through a 529 account, or investing in yourself through an online course.

Even if you're in the process of paying down debt, that is a form of investing since decreasing debt is increasing your net worth.

And regarding setting up investment accounts, it's easier than ever today. Setting up an IRA with Betterment is SO easy. super low fees, and there's no minimum. you can literally start with $5.

Tip # 147

Your children won't be emotionally harmed if you don't take them to Disney every year

There is a massive wealth transfer occurring in this country from broke, debt-shackled families to the massive empire that is Walt Disney World. Their marketing is amazing, and parents have bought into the hype hook, line, and sinker.

Your children do not need to experience Disney World. Sure, it's magical, they will have a blast, and you love seeing their faces light up upon seeing Mickey Mouse. But you've got to count the cost here. It might be the most expensive vacation that you can take. If you're in debt up to your eyeballs, going to Disney is a great way to keep you there.

Tip # 148

Your children won't be emotionally harmed if you don't get them iPhones

Growing up, imagine if you had all of the world's knowledge at your fingertips? It would have sounded like science fiction, right? But with smartphones, that's our world today.

And if you have children (especially children over the age of 11 or 12), most of their friends probably have smartphones. Now look – we're not going to get into a discussion of whether adolescents should have smartphones and access to social media, we're just going to carefully point out that they do not NEED them.

Shelling out $500+ per child every couple years just so that they can have an up-to-date gadget isn't the best use of money. Either make them pay for it or give them an old-school flip phone.

Tip # 149

You don't need to buy all organic food and shop at whole foods
These days, there is so much pressure on parents. On any given day, our Facebook, Instagram, and Pinterest feeds will show us dozens of pictures of 100% raw, organic, cage-free, GMO-free meals that other parents have prepared for their families.
You know exactly what I'm talking about.
Don't let it get to you. You can feed your children and family a very healthy diet without spending $5 per pound on chicken breast at Whole Foods. You have so many options.
Firstly, many foods really have no benefit to having the label organic. Secondly, you have other options besides grocery stores. Look into buying local meat. Each year, we buy a half of a cow from a local farm, and the price works out to be less than $4 a pound after being butchered.
Lastly – check out ALDI. They've got a huge and growing selection of organic foods. Being pressured to shop at the most expensive grocery stores to buy the best organic food might be keeping you poor.

Tip # 150

Once you get a raise, then everything won't be fine
Do you really believe that an extra $10,000 a year from a job will make a difference?
Wrong. You may be were so accustomed to spending every single dollar you take home, that it won't make the difference in your budget that you thought it would.
Making more money is great. But if your spending habits don't change too, then you will still be broke.

Tip # 151

You can't afford to give to charity
We get it. Money is tight. And you aren't sure if there's going to be anything left over after you pay the bills.
But guess what? No matter how bad you have it, someone else has it much worse. What you might consider a small amount of money is a very large sum of many in many parts of the world.

Giving isn't just good for the recipient. Giving is good for you. Giving makes you wealthy in ways that matter so much more than finances. And whether you believe in God or a higher power, we truly believe that those who are generous have more opportunity and wealth given to them.
If we believe that you can't afford to give, then that is keeping you poor.

Tip # 152

You are stuck in your current financial situation
There are two ways of looking at the world.
Some believe, whether they admit it or not, that all available money in the economy is a pie, and each person is allotted a small slice. If you have a job, that's your slice. Your paycheck is what you get, and you've got to make your budget and all your living expenses fit within those confines.
Others don't see the world this way. Money and finances are more fluid and if you want to make more money, you can go out and do it. You are not allotted just a small slice of the pie. Take as much as you want! And that doesn't mean you are taking from someone else; the pie can simply get bigger. There are so many ways to make extra money. You can switch careers later in life, you can work side jobs, or you can start a business. Sometimes those side jobs and little businesses making money from home end up completely replacing your normal paycheck. Your current paycheck is not the only money available to you. You are not stuck. Limiting yourself and your potential is keeping you poor.

Tip # 153

Your job is terrible
You feel underpaid, underappreciated, and overworked. And then you are passed up for that promotion. Oh, and that guy who got the promotion that you felt you deserved? Do you want to know something about him? I bet you $100 that he doesn't hate his job. I bet he might enjoy it.

The number one self-sabotaging career mistake is to hate your job. Gossip, a bad attitude, and a sense of entitlement are the results. And trust me, even if you think you are doing a good job keeping it to yourself, it's not a secret.

But this is something that you can change. Only you have control over your attitude at work.

But your job might not be a good fit, or your superiors are awful. Let's face it, some jobs really do suck, this one might not be a lie all the time. But if that's the case, then why are you still there? Develop an exit strategy and find a better fit. You'll be happier, and probably make much more money in the long run.

Tip # 154

Your home is an investment

Many believe that their home is their most asset. But it's more of a liability. Unless you buy and sell homes for a living, a home should not be treated as an investment; it should simply be treated as the place that you live. If you view it as an investment, it might just set you up for the poor house.

Historically, the value of residential real estate has provided a return right at the rate of inflation. But it's been much more volatile. Remember the early-mid 2000's when everyone was going crazy buying expensive homes because it was a great investment in addition to a place to live? Didn't end so well, did it?

The stock market has fluctuations too… but it's a different animal altogether when it's your dwelling place. If your home suddenly loses 20% of its value and puts you underwater, you're stuck. Physically stuck… as in, you can't move. You can either ride it out and wait for the value to increase, or lock in the loss and sell your home (but you might have to come up with a bunch of cash).

If your 401k portfolio loses 20% of its value, it sucks, but it doesn't really affect your living situation.

Purchasing a home as an investment instead of a dwelling usually results in bad choices. You will likely buy a more expensive house than you need, you won't have much of a down payment, and you are putting yourself through unnecessary risk.

Smaller house = More wealth.

Tip # 155

Constant interruptions

We are very unproductive if we keep our phones next to us while working, or if we open our favorite chat apps like Viber and Slack. Now, even when you have your colleagues on Slack, you want to work without being interrupted every few minutes.

So, turn off all chat apps, email notifications, and silence your phone. You will be surprised how fast you can complete tasks when no one and nothing can interrupt you.

EPIC ONE LINERS

Loadthispin.com

1) Knowledge is knowing a tomato is a fruit. Wisdom is not putting a tomato in a fruit salad.

2) The early bird might get the worm, but the second mouse gets the cheese.

3) Children: You spend the first two years of their life teaching them how to walk and talk. The next sixteen? Spent telling them to sit down and shut up.

4) He who smiles in a crisis has found someone to blame.

5) My mother never realized the irony in calling me a son-of-a-bitch.

6) Politicians and diapers have one thing in common. They should both be changed regularly, and for the same reason.

7) I thought I wanted a career, turns out I just wanted paychecks.

8) Sex is not the answer. Sex is the question. "Yes" is the answer.

9) If I agreed with you, we'd both be wrong.

10) To steal ideas from one person is plagiarism. To steal from many is research.

11) I asked God for a bike, but I know God doesn't work that way. So I stole a bike and asked for forgiveness.

12) Light travels faster than sound. This is why some people appear bright until you hear them speak.

13) We live in a society where pizza gets to your house faster than the police.

14) A bus station is where a bus stops. A train station is where a train stops. On my desk, I have a work station.

15) I should've known it wasn't going to work out between my ex-wife and me. After all, I'm a Libra and she's a bitch.

16) How is it one careless match can start a forest fire, but it takes a whole box to start a campfire?

17) I didn't fight my way to the top of the food chain to be a vegetarian.

18) A computer once beat me at chess, but it was no match for me at kick boxing.

19) I saw a woman wearing a sweat shirt with "Guess" on it...so I said "Implants?"

20) The shinbone is a device for finding furniture in a dark room.

21) Good girls are bad girls that never get caught.

22) Laugh at your problems, everybody else does.

23) Crowded elevators smell different to midgets.

24) The main reason Santa is so jolly is because he knows where all the bad girls live.

25) Did you know that dolphins are so smart that within a few weeks of captivity, they can train people to stand on the very edge of the pool and throw them fish?

26) God must love stupid people. He made SO many.

27) I didn't say it was your fault. I said I was blaming you.

28) Fighting for peace is like fucking for virginity.

29) Women will never be equal to men until they can walk down the street with a bald head and a beer gut, and still think they are sexy.

30) Always borrow money from a pessimist. He won't expect it back.

31) Some people say "If you can't beat them, join them". I say "If you can't beat them, beat them", because they will be expecting you to join them, so you will have the element of surprise.

32) Never hit a man with glasses. Hit him with a baseball bat.

33) We have enough gun control. What we need is idiot control.

34) A diplomat is someone who can tell you to go to hell in such a way that you will look forward to the trip.

35) Money can't buy happiness, but it sure makes misery easier to live with.

36) Some cause happiness wherever they go. Others... whenever they go.

37) I discovered I scream the same way whether I'm about to be devoured by a great white shark or if a piece of seaweed touches my foot.

38) I don't trust anything that bleeds for five days and doesn't die.

39) War does not determine who is right. It determines who is left.

Tip # 157

TV

We used to work and watch TV simultaneously. We justified it by saying that it didn't bother us, and we did not want to work in silence at home.

The fact is TV slows you down completely. And it is also very addicting, so one episode can soon become two or even four.

We would not get anything done if we continued to watch TV all night, so we completely changed this habit.

We occasionally watch TV, but we devote most of this time to taking care of our clients.

Tip # 158

Car payments

If you had to pick one single monthly cost that is wreaking havoc on your finances and making you broke, it is the car payment. It is killing us. The average car payment on a new car is almost $500. a month. We're convinced that car payments are the biggest thief of middle-class wealth in America.

Almost everyone we know has at least one car payment. We know that you need a car. You got to get to work. But if you're making car payments, I can guarantee that the car you financed is too expensive for your budget. You may feel wealthy driving it around, but it's making you broke.

Make your current vehicle the LAST vehicle that you finance. Then save up cash and buy a used car. It will take time, but your future will thank you.

Tip # 159

You need a bigger house

In 1973, the average size of a new home was 1,525 square feet. In 2015, it was 2,687. That's a dramatic increase, folks. And if you look at these stats per family member, it's even more dramatic given today's smaller family size.

The average living space per person in 1973 was 507 square feet... in 2015, 971. That's right, almost double.

You don't need a bigger house and the accompanying bigger mortgage payment. You might just need less stuff. And please stop calling that house you're in right now a starter home. It doesn't have to be. Smaller house = more wealth.

Tip # 160

 Survival Tips

#1

If you find a hair in your food, heavily salt it before sending it back to the kitchen to make sure you got a new order.

#2

If you ever get a flat tire, take a picture of it on your phone so for future reference you can use it as a valid excuse.

#3

If you're too embarrassed to buy something, get a birthday card with it.

#4

When in an argument, act as if you're being recorded. This will prevent you from saying stupid things you don't mean

#5

Always check your cell signal when looking for new apartments or dorms to live in.

#6

When you're finished with an essay, copy and paste it into Google Translate and listen to it. It's the easiest way to find mistakes.

Tip # 161

Don't place blame for past events
If you are in a difficult conversation with someone and he or she brings up a painful event from the past that is causing the current reaction, try not to explain away the problem. The pain is there, and you can either choose to help this person through it or choose to leave the conversation/relationship accordingly.
The pain isn't this person's fault. There may be nothing (s)he could have done differently in the past to have helped that situation; but even if there was, there is no changing the outcome now. You can only decide together how to move forward. There is no sense placing blame for past events.

Tip # 162

Sometimes it's best to simply listen
Another lesson we can all put into practice. Not every problem needs an immediate solution. Sometimes it's best to simply process the current experience in order to work through it. While advice, personal experience, and solutions may be helpful at some point down the line, it isn't always what is best in the present moment. We all need to learn to actively listen to the person we are speaking with. Hear this person out; genuinely consider her/his feelings and pain. Identify the message beyond the words.

Tip # 163

Checking emails
Now, we all must check emails multiple times per day, but do we need to do it constantly? Use your schedule to set time-blocks when you want to check your email. Do it three times per day: once in the morning when you wake up, once at 1 pm and one last time at 8 pm. It is important to stop checking emails all day long so that you can focus on more important tasks and not get interrupted.

Tip # 164

Online shopping

Online shopping is now one of the biggest time wasters for everyone. While it is convenient to just click and order whatever you want, it is so easy to start working and then click away to check something job related.

Now, let's be honest, we will not stop online shopping any time soon, but it is important to do it when you set aside some free time. Adopting a minimalistic lifestyle also helps. We find that we do not shop half as often as we used to, just because we do not want to pile on things we do not need. And we also want to save money.

Tip # 165

Create a Schedule

Setting up a new schedule for yourself can be a great way to succeed at your goals. Will you start going for a morning walk? You can always set your alarm twenty minutes earlier so that you have time to do it! Something more complex may require more adjustment of your current schedule, but you can fit anything in that you put your mind to.

We prioritize those things that mean the most to us.

15
FRUGAL HABITS
TO LIVE BY

1. Think long-term
2. Pay your future-self first
3. Live in a modest home
4. Use everything to the last drop
5. Look for deals and clip coupons
6. Quality instead of quantity
7. Enjoy staying at home
8. Cook food at home
9. Have an emergency fund
10. Repair and reuse
11. Don't shop for entertainment
12. Use a credit card with good rewards
13. Carry just enough cash with you
14. Drive a safe and reliable car
15. Don't buy lotto tickets

2017 BUDGET BINDER
PRINTABLES

MINTNOTION.COM

Tip # 167

Use a Habit Tracker

Have you ever tried tracking your habit progress? There are so many fun ways to do this! Tracking your habits gives you a great visual of your effort. This is especially good for those new habits that are going to take a lot more determination to make happen. You can also create step-goals that slowly increase the change as time goes on.

Tip # 168

Find Self-Motivation

Stay mindful of your thoughts. What is this change for? It better be for you! If you keep focused on what your motivation is, you will be more likely to relentlessly pursue these new goals!
Inspiration boards can be a huge help to keep yourself focused, but you can also create little rewards for yourself. For example, for every five pounds you lose there is a new workout outfit you can purchase to boost your confidence!

Tip # 169

Join a Support Group / Community

Communities can be incredibly supportive of new changes for its members. Find a person or a community that you can check in with. This will keep you accountable for your successes and struggles. People can also give you supportive advice to keep you on track as well. We are social creatures, and creatures of habit–so seek help when you need it.

Tip # 170

Stay Flexible

Not every habit is built overnight, and not all goals are met within a week, month, or even a year! Be patient with yourself and stay appreciative of any and all progress you make. It is very common that people will trip up and falter on new goals. This is normal. The important part is that you choose to keep moving forward; you choose success.

Tip # 171

Make a SMART goal

What is a SMART goal? It's a specific, measurable, attainable, relevant, and time-bound goal.

To make sure your goals are clear and reachable, each one should be:
Specific (simple, sensible, significant).
Measurable (meaningful, motivating).
Achievable (agreed, attainable).
Relevant (reasonable, realistic and resourced, results-based).

Time bound (time-based, time limited, time/cost limited, timely, time-sensitive).

Tip # 172

Break it Down

Some goals are amazing ideas and can be significantly healthier for you! But deciding you want to go vegan overnight, for example, isn't the best route for many people. You would need to be driven by some powerful decision-making powers to make it happen.
A more sustainable idea would be to decide to stop eating meat the first month of the year, then eggs the following month, drop dairy the following month, and go down to the smaller animal-derived ingredients from there. This breaks the larger goal into smaller ones—and allows you less stress, providing more opportunity for success.

Tip # 173

Advice isn't always warranted

Maybe you hate to see those you love struggling. You hate it so much that you will often try to tell them what other options there are or what else might be done to improve the situation.

But at the end of the day, you aren't in this person's shoes. Perhaps there are times when advice is warranted—or is simply required based on the situation and those involved—but in general you should save advice for when it is sought out. In general, you will find that if someone isn't asking for your advice, this person isn't in the mindset to accept the advice. By giving it anyway, you risk adding to the frustration of the conversation.

Tip # 174

Maybe the bright side doesn't matter

A difficult conversation comes up, and rather than facing it full force you will attempt to throw in, **"Well, at least…."** This is to decrease the intensity of the conversation.

But depending on how this is used, it can be taken as excusing the issue if you are at fault or attempting to minimize the issue at hand. It also can really damage the feelings of the other person as well, as the person may feel as if his/her pain isn't warranted. None of these things you intend to do during your conversation with this person, and yet it still may happen.

Tip # 175

Try not to take all things personally

There are some struggles you may have caused or added to. Some situations are your fault. However, not everything has to do with you.

The person you are having a conversation with may have an existing mindset in a certain situation that will cause them to react a certain way. There may be nothing you can do to trigger a better result. Sometimes, you simply must ride out the struggle together—and try to reassure the other person until (s)he feels secure again.

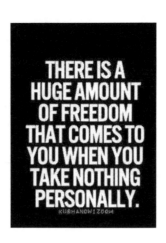

THERE IS A
HUGE AMOUNT
OF FREEDOM
THAT COMES TO
YOU WHEN YOU
TAKE NOTHING
PERSONALLY.
KUSHANDWIZDOM

Tip # 176

Remember, feelings cannot be "wrong." We find that many people attempt to do this during conversations. One person will share true feelings about how a situation made him/her feel, and because the other person feels guilty or isn't sure how to help, he or she will reject it all together. We need to be sensitive of the feelings of others. Just because you did not intend for your actions to affect the other person's feelings in that way does not mean that the pain isn't valid. Rather than saying, **"Well that's not what I meant,"** or something similar, try, **"I'm sorry that doing ___ made you feel that way. I did not mean to hurt you."** At that point you can explain your side, but you should only do so after ensuring you've addressed the person's feelings first.

It doesn't matter what your intentions were if you still hurt someone else. Still address the feelings at hand before explaining your true intentions.

Tip # 177

Plan Ahead

You can start goals at any time of the year, but today is the day to set the date you're going all in. The trick to achieving your goals is choosing success because even if you trip along the way, if you chose to be successful you will keep pushing forward.

Once you have decided when you will start you will be able to plan your way to success! Are there any ways you can prepare for the journey? If you're going to eat clean, do you have a shopping list prepared and your fridge cleaned out? Start planning today!

IDEAS FOR PRACTICING

SELF-CARE

PHYSICAL

go for a walk
dance
hike
swim
get a hug
play with a dog
clean & reorganize your room
take a bath

MENTAL

read a book
learn a new skill like photography or drawing
do a DIY project
color
turn your phone off

EMOTIONAL

meditate
practice Yoga
light a candle
talk with a friend
go on a date
journal
write down a list of things you're grateful for

Tip # 178

They are always improving their skills
Part of being successful means you are always learning new things. You are always improving your skills or learning a new skill. Successful work at home moms are always reading a new book on how to grow their business or increase their income.
As a mom business owner, you have many options to learn new skills. You can read books, listen to podcasts, and take online courses. To grow your skills and your business, you want to always be learning. We always have new business books to read. Whenever we have a few minutes, we should pull one out and read a few chapters.

Tip # 179

They focus on one project at a time
We would all like to believe we are multi-taskers. But, we can only focus on one task at a time.
Choose your biggest most important project and focus on it with your full attention. Don't try to work on multiple tasks at one time. Having all the windows on your computer open at one time seems great until, you email the wrong file to an important client, miss conference calls and meetings and forget basic tasks.
Stay focused and focus on one important thing at a time.

Tip # 180

They allow margin time
We all need margin time. Margin time allows us to handle the unexpected. Your computer won't start, your file won't save, you lost an important report, your child is sick and needs you right this minute. Margin time means you have a little extra time and won't be stressed when the unexpected happens.
How much margin time do you need? Daily, 15 minutes to 1 hour would be great. If you are planning a big project or have client deadlines, allow 1-2 days of margin time. If you complete the project early, you will have an extra day to recheck or proofread before sending to your client.

If you always feel rushed and stressed, you probably need more margin time in your day.

Tip # 181

They set goals

Setting goals are vital for maintaining your focus. You need your goals to help you zone in on your target.

The times when we set clear goals and a deadline for completion are the times we am most focused and know exactly what we need to do accomplish each day.

Goals also show you how far you have come. As you see your progress, you will be encouraged to work harder to reach your longer-term goals too.

If you don't have goals, you will eventually get lost and start to wonder why you started your business. Don't let that be you. Set your goals now.

Tip # 182

They avoid distractions

Distractions, distractions, they are everywhere. When we are working on our business, we need blinders.

Think about a horse in a race. They put blinders on the horse, so the horse will focus on just it's race and no other distractions. You need the same laser focus with no distractions on your business.

Tips for Social Media

Focus on 1 or 2 platforms that benefit your business most

Have set times you share content

Preschedule content if possible

Set a timer and time limit for each platform

(15 minutes for Facebook, 20 minutes for Pinterest)

You only have 3 -4 hours to work on my business each day. To keep your business growing, you must stay focused and avoid all unnecessary distractions.

Social Media, Internet, Games

No doubt this is one of the biggest time-wasters. While it is nice to keep up with friends and know what they are doing, social media is now much more than that. We are following people we do not know, we are clicking on ads, and it is all so addictive.

.

Without even noticing, you can spend hours scrolling through your Instagram feed, checking Facebook, or reading the latest Tweets. Our biggest time wasters used to be YouTube and Facebook. We can spend hours "working" and listening to YouTube videos. This habit got so out of control that we think we spent around 4-5 hours per day just watching videos.

Once we managed to reduce that time, we suddenly felt so much better and we could get so many things done. So be honest and see how much time you spend on social media and the internet. Replace your binge-watching with writing goals or some other worthy effort.

Tip # 183

They set a specific time for work
If you want to be successful working at home, you need a specific work time. You can't show up late, or worse be a no show. You must have a set time to work on your business. It can be a different time on different days, but you must commit to a set time every day.

If you just say, I need to work on my business today, before you know it your day will be gone, and you got busy, but did not work on your business and goals.

Grab your favorite calendar (print or electronic), start blocking the time on your calendar that you will spend working on your business. You must commit to be consistent.

Successful business owners work on their business daily and they don't skip the hard stuff. You are a successful work at mom or dad too, so start planning.

Tip # 184

They are focused

Work at home moms or fathers have limited time to work on their businesses. They are working during nap time, after their children go to bed, or early in the morning hours. So, to be successful, no minute can be wasted. You need focus!

Don't be discouraged if you were not born with great focus. You can learn to be more focused. In fact, most of the steps like avoiding distractions, setting goals and working on one project at a time are all about staying focused.

First, start with determining what you want to focus on. Get a vision of what you want your business to be in one month, 6 months, 1 year and 5 years. Now, decide what you need to do to be focused on making your business reach each of these goals.

Tip # 185

They make time for hobbies

Successful people know that they need to take occasional breaks from the hard driving work ethic.

Making time for a hobby allows the mind to rest from the constant work, work, work mindset. Doing something other than work regularly is good for mental health.

Successful habits are the foundation of a well-lived life. Follow the ways of those already on top and learn from their successes and mistakes. Start working to adopt these 15 amazing ways to be more successful in your everyday life.

A smart approach to becoming successful is to start by picking one or maybe two of these traits to work on.

Tip # 186

They give back and help others

Along with being grateful, successful people appreciate the blessings that they have received in life and are willing to share their successes by giving to those in need.

Successful people understand the importance of helping others and how giving back also helps them too.

Tip # 187

Tip # 188

They make time for family and friends

Maintaining connections and relationships with relatives and friends supports their personal support network. A strong family support network is invaluable to successful people.

Successful people are working hard toward achieving their goals and need to take time to celebrate their accomplishments with loved ones.

They take time to nurture and nourish family support networks.

Some people will
never like you.
Because your
spirit irritates
their demons.

They are self-aware

Successful people are confident in their abilities and are self-aware of their strengths and weaknesses.

Successful people don't blame others for any failures, they just accept their failures and learn from them and grow.

They focus on their strengths and what they are good at. They also will minimize their weaknesses.

Tip # 191

They read regularly

A trait that is common among successful people is they are always in a learning mode. They consume massive amounts of information by reading regularly.

People who are successful will credit their success to the fact they were constantly seeking knowledge to become better and more effective at their business and personal life.

Continuous learning is one of the amazing ways to be more successful in your everyday life.

Tip # 192

They let go of the past

If you want to be a successful person, you have a clear mind and clear vision. Focus on your work, build discipline, don't get distracted.

In order to keep your vision in mind, you will need to let go of the past and focus on the future.

You can't build the healthy successful habits if you are comparing your current time to your past.

By looking back, you are reliving it all over again and taking a step backwards from your desired goals.

Make room your new habits and let a positive transformation take over your life.

Tip # 193

Drink more water

Our body needs water daily, but most people aren't drinking enough each day. Drinking water helps your skin and helps to maintain regularity in the body.

Make an effort to drink fewer soft drinks and drink more water daily. If you don't drink water, you will die. It's that important. Depending on our environment, we can live only a few days without water - maybe a week. We can live much longer without food. For most of us, we should prioritize the consumption of water far more than we currently do.

Water can Prevent cancer. Yes, that's right – various research says staying hydrated can reduce risk of colon cancer by 45%, bladder cancer by 50%, and possibly reduce breast cancer risk as well.

You will be less cranky. Research says dehydration can affect your mood and make you grumpy and confused. Think clearer and be happier by drinking more water.

Water can help you to perform better. Proper hydration contributes to increased athletic performance. Water composes 75% of our muscle tissue! Dehydration can lead to weakness, fatigue, dizziness, and electrolyte imbalance.

You can lose weight by drinking water. Sometimes we think we are hungry, when we are thirsty. Our body just starts turning on all the alarms when we ignore it. For those of you trying to drop some pounds, staying hydrated can serve as an appetite suppressant and help with weight loss.

You can also have less joint pain if you drink water. Drinking water can reduce pain in your joints by keeping the cartilage soft and hydrated. This is how glucosamine helps reduce joint pain, by aiding in cartilage's absorption of water.

Flush out waste and bacteria. Our digestive system needs water to function properly. Waste is flushed out in the form of urine and sweat. If we don't drink water, we don't flush out waste and it collects in our body causing a myriad of problems. Also combined with fiber, water can cure constipation.

Prevent headaches. Sometimes headaches can be caused by dehydration, so drinking water can prevent or alleviate that nasty head pain. Next time your head hurts, try drinking water.

Make your skin glow. Our skin is the largest organ in our body. Regular and plentiful water consumption can improve the color and texture of your skin by keeping it building new cells properly. Drinking water also helps the skin do its job of regulating the body's temperature through sweating.

Feed your body. Water is essential for the proper circulation of nutrients in the body. Water serves at the body's transportation system and when we are dehydrated things just can't get around as well.

Tip # 194

They exercise regularly

Regular exercise is not only good for your body, but it also helps with mental clarity. Exercise also helps with your energy and focus as well.

In order to be more productive, start your day with a workout. If you only exercise for 20 minutes, jump starting your body will help you jump start your day.

Tip # 195

They take risks

Successful people do not let their fears keep them from achieving their goals. They are willing to take risks to pursue their dreams and be successful.

If you want to develop successful habits, you will need to become a risk taker.

All high achievers know how to take risks and get out of their comfort zones to do something to achieve their goals.

Tip # 196

They stay in their lane

Because successful people are so focused on achieving their goals, they don't worry about what other people around them are doing. They also don't spend time comparing themselves to others or their competition.

They always seek to be better and their indicator for their progress is to review their own progress against their goal. An Olympic athlete is a good example. Most Olympic athletes are working to get better against their own performance goals.

Tip # 197

They are consistent

Being consistent is major trait that is common among successful people. You must be consistent to succeed at anything.

If you work to devote your time and focus on a task and be consistent in your efforts, you will see results.

Tip # 198

They focus on their most important tasks first
Another essential trait included in the amazing ways to be more successful in your everyday life is focusing on what is important. By planning your day on the night before allows you to focus on the most important tasks that you need to get done.
Each night make a list of the tasks that you need to complete the next morning. Make those tasks your priority the moment you wake up. Don't get sidetrack with unimportant things that will keep you from accomplishing your most important tasks.

Tip # 199

They have a vision for their life
All successful people have a vision and a well thought out plan to achieve their goals in their life.
People who are successful know exactly what they want to achieve, and they develop a detailed plan for getting there.
So many people aimlessly go through life with no vision for their life. Without a vision, they keep doing the same things year after year.
If you want to be successful in your life, you will need to develop a vision for it. Having a vision for your life is one of the most essential traits for amazing ways to be more successful in your everyday life.

Tip # 200

life
hacks

Have a migraine? Put your hands in ice water a flex them several times... Headache gone!

#997
1000LifeHacks.com

Made in the USA
Columbia, SC
09 February 2025

53556706R10076